W9-BNE-365

ACRL Publications in Librarianship no. 53

People Come First:
User-Centered
Academic Library Service

Edited by

Dale S. Montanelli

&

Patricia F. Stenstrom

Association of College and Research Libraries
A division of the American Library Association
Chicago 1999

The paper used in this publication meets the minimum requirements of American National Standard for Information Sciences–Permanence of Paper for Printed Library Materials, ANSI Z39.48—1992.∞

Library of Congress Cataloging-in-Publication Data
People come first : user-centered academic library service / edited by
    Dale S. Montanelli & Patricia F. Stenstrom.
        p. cm. -- (ACRL publications in librarianship ; no. 53)
    Includes bibliographical references and index.
    ISBN 0-8389-7999-8 (alk. paper)
    1. Academic libraries--United States. 2. Libraries and readers-
    -United States. I. Montanelli, Dale S. II. Stenstrom, Patricia.
    III. Series.
    Z674.A75 no. 53
    [Z675.U5]
    027.7--dc21   98-43719

Printed in the United States of America.

02 01 00 99   5 4 3 2 1

This book is dedicated to the memory of

Hugh C. Atkinson

who really did believe that people come first.

Acknowledgments

The authors wish to express their appreciation to
Stephen E. Wiberley Jr. for his editorial suggestions
and to Sandra Wolf of the UIUC Library and Information
Science Library for her assistance in "getting it right."

Table of Contents

Preface

We wanted to edit a book that emphasized service to users and that was written by librarians who had experience as practitioners. We did not reject any current management theory, but we also did not want to embrace any single approach. In addition, we wanted a book about service and not about technology. As it turned out, several authors found it challenging to write about user service because they were unaccustomed to looking at library functions from a user's point of view.

The book begins with two chapters that provide overviews of the issues at stake and then presents a discussion of particular activities. In the opening chapter, Michael Gorman introduces three themes that recur throughout the other chapters: the use of technology to empower users, the need to consult users in planning, and the importance of friendly, knowledgeable service. Lizabeth A. Wilson next offers a plan to provide high-quality service to a frequently ignored group of users—undergraduates. She emphasizes the importance of working with other campus groups to integrate the library into the infrastructure of the campus. She also encourages librarians to be advocates for their patrons and to embrace the diversity of the audiences served.

The chapters that follow are written from a functional perspective, but the overlapping nature of the services is still evident. In fact, each author strays across functional boundaries to describe future visions of library service and new collaborative relationships within the library. All the chapters stress the interdependence of the formerly discrete functional units in meeting user information needs. For instance, Patricia F. Stenstrom suggests that the cataloger of the future will be a public service librarian and that the functions of cataloging and reference will merge. The distinctions among services and their locations are increasingly unimportant. The challenge for librarians is to make finding information for any library user a seamless process.

Technology and teaching are presented as tools for providing service. They support the movement away from the library as a place to the library as a service that is available wherever and whenever the user needs it. New approaches have reduced, or in some cases, eliminated the dependence on physical location for management of library processes.

Effective management systems for service-oriented libraries are those in which the outcomes for the user, rather than the means and the processes of the librarians, are emphasized. As Patricia A. McCandless and Dale S. Montanelli explain, the role of management is to give librarians the resources they need to achieve user-oriented service. Both of these authors offer some insights on how library managers can aid in the implementation of user-centered services.

We hope that readers will find these chapters thought-provoking and that the chapters will stimulate a dialogue on the role of service. If librarians are bold enough to risk change, the tools they have at their disposal will allow them to reshape library activities to better serve users.

Avoiding the Seven Deadly Sins

or

Technology and the Future of Library Service in Academic Libraries

Michael Gorman

It is to be all made of faith and service.
William Shakespeare, *As You Like It*

This paper is a small repayment of the immense personal and professional debt the author owes to the life, example, and teaching of his late friend and colleague Hugh C. Atkinson, a man who devoted his considerable gifts to improving library service in academic libraries. For the author, the epitome of Hugh's deep commitment to practical librarianship came when he said, a propos of bibliographic instruction, that "An ounce of help is worth a ton of instruction"—a sentiment that demonstrates perfectly his scorn for cant and his belief that libraries have been built on earth above all to help the people that use them in all the ways they need help. Those ways can include instruction if it is dedicated to empowering the library user.

In latter years, the author has found himself more and more interested in the concept of service in libraries. Decades ago, he started his career in libraries in the then thrice-blessed London public library system. It is true to say, then, that the idea of service as something separable from library work would have seemed quite preposterous, simply because service was what we were and what we did. However, academic libraries have been slow to come to that realization and have had to don the service ethic in recent times, rather than to have lived the

1

organic relationship between service and librarianship. Too many academic libraries and academic librarians have been transfixed by the solipsistic idea of the academic library as an entity that is because it is. Although there is a nobility in the idea of a great research library preserving the records of civilizations past and present, there is also the daily reality of millions of actual and potential library users who need training and assistance in the use of the stores of recorded knowledge and information that libraries have in their collections.

One difficult topic is that of the inverse relationship between size of library and service orientation. The author has labored in vineyards great and small and have observed that the smaller the collection and staff (and building, come to that), the more likely it is that service is the dominating factor. In all likelihood, it was this perception that made Hugh Atkinson such a strong proponent of specialized "departmental" and subject area libraries in the large academic libraries he headed. Despite the many logical, financial, and staffing problems that such systems generate, he probably was right in hewing to that belief. The facts are that large libraries are, almost inevitably, bureaucratized and that the nearer the deliverers of library services are to the recipients of those services, the more likely they are to be attuned to the real needs their services will satisfy.

Libraries are in the service business. The most important product they have is service. Without service, libraries are indistinguishable from museums or, in the vision of the French filmmaker Alain Resnais,[1] they are a combination of a maze and a morgue for books. Service is a pervasive ethic of the profession of librarianship. In an illuminating article, Lee Finks[2] lists "service" as the very first of the librarians "professional values."[3] In his words,

> we will gladly serve—not because we are trying to get rich or feel important and not because we are merely doing a job. . . . Two motivations are evident here: a need and an urge. . . . society has a need for libraries and librarianship . . . but we also serve because we choose to serve.

Librarianship, like other, similar professions, is characterized by the willingness of its practitioners to work for the general good with only small tangible reward. Again, in the words of Lee Finks,

It is, we should admit, a noble urge, this altruism of ours, one that seems both morally and psychologically good.

From the very earliest days of modern libraries, we see a selfless sentiment and a way of thinking that have been characterized by some as the "Angel in the House" syndrome that pervades all majority female professions.[4] Many contend that most women possess this selflessness to a greater degree than do most men—a sentiment with which the author agrees as he does with the suggestion that most women pull off the difficult trick of being simultaneously finer and more practical than most men. However it may be, the fact remains that librarians labor in a field—librarianship—that has as one of its dominant ethical beliefs the idea that, in being librarians, we are committed to service in the broadest sense. The broad purpose of librarianship is to collect, preserve, and disseminate "documents" (records of knowledge and information of all kinds—linear and nonlinear) and to provide training and assistance in the use of those documents. In doing these things, librarians serve humanity in a very direct and important way. Service, in the library context, can be as limited in scope as an individual act of thoughtfulness in helping a library user and can be as grand as playing a part in giving access to the records of civilization.

Although librarians are in the service business in a metaphorical sense, the fact remains that we are not a "business" as the word is generally understood, meaning that we must seek motivations other than profit for what we do. Service in the "for-profit" sector has a very simple motivation. It has been shown, time and again, that maximum service means maximum monetary reward. From Harrods to Nordstrom to Scandinavian Airlines to IBM to AAA, reliability, courtesy, and attention to the needs of the individual pay off handsomely.

Contrariwise, librarians dividends are neither so easily counted nor easily evaluated. The bottom line for a service-oriented librarian is the psychic satisfaction that accompanies a job well done and the knowledge that is buried somewhere in the consciousness of every librarian that even the most ordinary task in a library plays a part in the advancement of culture and civilization.

We have to establish the ethic of service as a central fact of our professional lives and to learn to apply that ethic in every aspect of our work. One way of learning how to apply the service ethic is to look to the lessons of the private for profit sector. This may come relatively easily to special librarians who work in that sector. It is, however, an approach that academic librarians have to learn to appreciate. Karl Albrecht, in his book *At America's Service,*[5] makes a passionate and compelling case for informing American business with "service management," a term he defines as "a total organizational approach that makes quality of service, *as perceived by the customer* [author's emphasis], the number one driving force for the operation of the business."[6] He describes this concept as one that is "transformational" for two basic reasons. First, it shifts the emphasis from other concerns to the single concern of satisfying the customer. Second, it is a total organizational approach that drives all the activities of the corporation. He points out that the typical American business either has a customer service department (which, when one thinks of it, implies that other branches of the company are not concerned with serving the customer) or simply waits until the level of complaint becomes unbearable, at which point some quick and easy solution (usually involving blaming the lower-level people who deal with the public directly) is implemented. Few libraries have a customer service department, though many circulation desks operate as such de facto. On the other hand, "management by reaction to complaints" is by no means uncommon in libraries.

How can this concept of service management be used to enable the library to become what Charles Martell has called "the client-centered library"?[7] The interest here is in the shift of emphasis and the psychological reorientation rather than in any specific organizational or administrative response. It is instructive to look at academic libraries that are successful in terms of user satisfaction and those that are not, and to seek to discern the factors that make them so. The author has, among others, worked for a national library—the British Library—and for a large academic library. They both had an ethic that was largely based on the size and depth of their collections, a belief that their very existence was self-justifying and quite separate from the use that was made of those collections or services that were provided to their users. For example, in an exchange overheard between a user of the then

British Museum Library (more properly Department of Printed Books) and one of the "Keepers" (a significant nomenclature in itself), the innocent asked for books on a certain subject. The reply, given in a grating Oxbridge drawl, was a magnificent: "We have no subject catalogue." End of conversation. The way in which many large academic libraries treat their undergraduate clients is nothing short of scandalous. However, it is true to say that most of the large academic libraries in this country went through a decades-long period in which collection building was their primary focus and that some of those libraries have not yet fully emerged from that phase. In other words, the transition from the Age of Collection Building to the Age of Service is not yet complete.

To turn to the brighter picture, any of us can name types of libraries that have, typically, very high levels of customer satisfaction. These service-oriented and highly successful libraries include almost all children's libraries, many special libraries, small public libraries (especially community branch libraries), and small college libraries. These libraries share certain obvious characteristics that differentiate them from others. The first is size. Smallness actually seems better in most areas of human endeavor, and in this instance, it provides an incalculably valuable asset—the opportunity for frequent personal interaction between librarians and their clientele. It is very difficult to take a cavalier attitude toward the library user community if it is a collection of known human beings rather than an abstraction. The other differentiating characteristic is that these libraries have both a clearly defined clientele and a clearly defined mission. It is likely that few children's librarians spend much time in a state of existential anxiety centered on their role in life. Any librarian who knows his or her customers and their needs, as well as his or her mission, is well on the way to becoming a service management success. Molière's M. Jourdain was amazed to discover that he had been speaking prose all his life.[8] It is quite possible that librarians in the institutions discussed here have been practicing the most modern service-oriented librarianship for decades without realizing how much in the vanguard they have been.

The besetting sin of librarianship is the confusing of means and ends. This reached its apogee in the form of the old-time cataloguers who, in their enthusiasm for rules and such, quite lost sight of the simple purpose of catalogues—the connection between book A and user B. Such confusion will kill service. A truly service-oriented library should have a clear view of its goals and purposes and a willingness to try new means and abandon old ones to achieve those goals and purposes. That concentration on means and indifference to ends is one of the pervasive themes of what Albrecht calls the "seven deadly sins of service." The other pervasive theme is that of people who work in institutions who have what is called nowadays "an attitude." The public sees that "attitude" only in the people with whom it comes into contact. However, this is not to say that only those people have an attitude problem. Indeed, it can be argued persuasively that it is the corporate culture that is at fault because it breeds, or at least allows, such negative and indifferent behavior. Service orientation has to come from the top and has to be incorporated into the minds and hearts of the institution as a whole. The argument here is not that we, as librarians, should succumb to a mindless group mentality, but rather, that we should come together, as individuals with different talents and responsibilities to work cooperatively to achieve the aims in which we all believe.

Albrecht's "seven deadly sins of service" are:[9]
- apathy;
- brush-off;
- coldness;
- condescension;
- robotism;
- rule book;
- runaround.

Can there be any librarian of experience who has not seen some or all of these sins being committed in an academic library?

Apathy is the result of a complete lack of service orientation, either because it has never been there or because of burnout. It manifests itself in many ways. A common example in bygone (it is hoped) days was that of the cataloguer who was completely indifferent to the fact that the card catalogue was user-hostile.

Brush-off is the result of the lack of personal involvement in the needs of the library's users. It can be seen in the librarian who gives only the most perfunctory answer to a reference question while knowing full well that the questioner has not formulated her or his need fully and clearly.

Coldness is the result of the lack of personal concern for the library's users as individuals. This is sometimes difficult to spot in colleagues or ourselves (though the library user senses it immediately) because it occurs most often in those librarians who "are good at their job." It is good to be efficient, but it is not good to prize efficiency above all and to deny library users the warmth and consideration they deserve.

Condescension arises from the feeling that we are somehow better than the average library user because we are more informed. It is foolish to look down on someone just because she or he knows less about the collections and services of libraries than we do. However, that foolishness is prevalent and demonstrable in some academic libraries.

Robotism arises from lack of imagination and creativity. It consists of devising a procedure and sticking to it regardless of circumstances. It should be remembered that robotism is often imposed on those in contact with the public by bad managers. For example, the author's daughter, then a first-year undergraduate at a major university, called the undergraduate library one miserable Midwestern night and asked if a book was available. The library, equipped with a comprehensive online system, refused to answer her question saying it was "library policy" that students had to come in to the library to consult the system themselves. Robotism of the first order!

Adherence to the *rule book* is similar to robotism in that it is a refuge of the unimaginative and insecure. Even more than robotism, the fault of the management of the library who will have failed to instill a sense of the *ends* to which a process is dedicated. A classic example of this sin is to be found in the library and librarians who make the collection of fines an end in itself rather than a means to encourage the return of materials (their only real purpose).

Runaround is due to the lack of commitment to individual service. It consists of passing the buck on all possible occasions, of asking people to wait an inordinate time for the service they want, and of imposing an inordinate delay in the delivery of service in order to make your own life easier. S. R. Ranganathan, in his unjustly neglected *Five Laws of Library Science*, says "Save the time of the reader [library user]."[10] He does *not* say "save the time of the cataloguer/reference librarian/etc."

How can these deadly sins be avoided? Most obviously, we can change our attitudes and the orientation of our libraries. It may be naive to think so, but individual commitments to change can make a difference and even the most entrenched bureaucracies and dim bulb bosses can be overcome by the power of belief. In this sense, technology is not the answer but, rather, is a tool that can be used to create the library in which the service ethic is paramount. Library technology, *intelligently applied*, can be used in concert with new service-oriented attitudes to achieve a great deal.

This technology contains, but is not limited to:

- integrated online systems that bring together and make accessible all the information the library has about itself;
- online systems used as "gateways" to a multitude of electronic databases (bibliographic, numeric, graphic, and full text);
- automated library instruction;
- remote access to library collections and services;
- interactive video technology;
- using computer and video techniques for storage and retrieval of texts (especially journal articles);
- provision of electronic documents;
- linkage to other library and nonlibrary systems;
- provision of access to bibliographic and nonbibliographic databases.

It is worth noting here that the service ethic will mandate the involvement, by some means or other, of the library user in the design of such technological projects. This can be accomplished in various ways—surveys, open meetings, individual consultations, appointments to committees, etc.—but if we are truly to serve the library user, we had better make sure that the product we are producing is one that she or he wants.

All of these technological applications are concerned with the *empowerment* of the library user because they are all means of maximizing the citizen's access to knowledge and information that will make her or his life better or more bearable or more fun. It is also a textbook case of the continuing history of the evolution of librarianship in that it consists, in many instances, of removing the librarian from the interaction of library user and library materials. It was ever thus—open stacks, public catalogues, open reference collections (up to and including CD-ROM indexes), etc., all are means to allow unfettered access to the library's collections and services. This greater degree of freedom of access does not in any way diminish the role of the librarian. On the contrary, it frees librarians from often unproductive activities so they can focus on direct personal interaction in situations in which such interaction is fruitful. The librarian of tomorrow will serve the library user in three ways:

1. by designing and improving systems that allow more and more access to knowledge and information;
2. by removing her- or himself from situations in which the user can interact directly with the collections and/or systems;
3. by being available to act as a guide, philosopher, and friend at times when such a role is needed and productive.

How can technology be used to avoid the Seven Deadly Sins? All that follows is based on the idea that, as a precondition, we will have altered our fundamental attitudes and become focused on the satisfaction of our customers—the users of the library. Moreover, the academic library administration has to build a working environment in which the commitment to service can flourish and in which a lack of such commitment is identified and corrected immediately. Given such changes, here are some things that can be done with technology.

Apathy. We can and should create user-friendly systems not systems that just have cute names and that introduce themselves with some inanity ("Hi! My name is Peaches and I'll be your friendly library system today!"), but rather, systems that have been designed from the beginning to satisfy the needs of the user and in which the exigencies of library work are always subordinated to usability. We can also use systems to create the kind of interest and excitement in the library staff that will preclude apathy.

Brush-off. Used intelligently, library technology will eliminate or greatly reduce the amount of busy work that librarians and staff have to do. Those employees (professional and others) will then be able to concentrate on the more important and fulfilling aspects of their jobs. This, in turn, will bring about an increase in personal security and job satisfaction that will make it very unlikely that the brush-off will be a common response to a user's request.

Coldness. A technologically advanced library in which the employees feel valued, secure in their worth to the library, and not overwhelmed by trivial pursuits will be, of its nature, a warm place. Self-esteem, that much-ridiculed preoccupation of many Californians, is intimately connected to feeling valuable to individuals and society in one's working life. The combination of user-friendly systems and user-directed, confident librarians will raise library service to new heights.

Condescension. This is, of course, the ultimate attitudinal problem. However, if the intelligent use of technology creates a climate in which the librarian is in partnership with the library user, it is a problem that will simply cease to exist. In addition, to design effective user-friendly systems, the librarian has to put her- or himself in the place of the user and essentially view the system through the eyes of that user. It is hard to retain condescension if one has gone through that experience.

Robotism. One of the attractive by-products of automation is the reduction of unnecessary rigidity and repetition. The systems should allow the librarian to work in an atmosphere of flux and change in which it is possible to come up with creative responses to individual circumstances. It would seem that only a robot could be robotic under those conditions.

Who needs a *rule book* when the rules are few, clear, and short? The combination of cumbersome manual systems and barnacled bureaucracy has led to a situation in which those who delight in applying rules without regard to their utility have flourished. The clean breeze of automation and the bracing effect of loosening bureaucratic structures will do away with the need for "rule books." Those who are temperamentally unsuited to working without the reinforcement and false security of complex and rigid rules will, in all probability, seek other spheres of work.

Runaround. It seems that we should be planning a new kind of library, one that does away with the fragmentation of the past and one in which there is a seamless web of service to the library user. If all the systems in the library are integrated and interactive and if the organizational structures of the library are built around those systems, there will be no opportunity to give a library user the "runaround." In addition, the personal satisfaction that comes from the efficient delivery of service will reduce the desire to hand off a user to someone else.

Three things are necessary to create the service-oriented academic library of the future. They are:

- vision;
- attitudinal change;
- user-friendly systems.

The vision has to come from the leadership of the library, which also has to support and encourage the changes in orientation and attitudes that these times demand. The library's systems are a means of carrying out the vision and the orientation toward service. A system without vision and commitment has no soul. On the other hand, no amount of vision and commitment can compensate for the lack of transforming systems to carry them into effect. Librarians should be neither dilettantes concerned with the ideal nor technocrats concerned only with machines. The future of academic librarianship lies in the marriage of vision and practical innovation using every available technology.

Notes

1. *Toute la mémorie du monde* (1956).

2. Lee Finks, "Values without Shame," *American Libraries* (Apr. 1989):352–56.

3. The others are stewardship, philosophical values, democratic values, and reading and books.

4. See, for example, Dee Garrison, *Apostles of Culture: The Public Librarian and American Society* (New York: Free Pr., 1979).

5. Karl Albrecht, *At America's Service: How Corporations Can Revolutionize the Way They Treat Their Customers* (Homewood, Ill.: Dow Jones-Irwin, 1988). The author wishes to acknowledge his debt to Mimi Drake, whose paper at the Second LITA National Conference published as "Don't Promise What You Can't Deliver," in *Convergence: Proceedings of the Second National Conference of the Library and Information Technology Association, October 2–6, 1988, Boston* (Chicago: ALA, 1990), 268–70 first brought Karl Albrecht's book and ideas to his attention.

6. Ibid., 20.

7. Charles Martell, *The Client-Centered Academic Library: An Organizational Model* (Westport, Conn.: Greenwood Pr., 1983).

8. Molière, *Le bourgeois gentilhomme*, II, iv, 1670.
> M. Jourdain: "Par ma foi! Il y a plus de quarante ans que je
> dis de la prose sans que j'en susse rien."

9. Albrecht, *At America's Service.*

10. S. R. Ranganathan, *The Five Laws of Library Science*, 2nd ed. (Madras: Madras Library Association; London: Blunt and Sons, 1957).

The Gateway Library:
Rethinking Undergraduate Services

Lizabeth A. Wilson

> The librarian must be ready to support the teacher in
> promoting the student's mastery of working heuristics of
> problem solving and for this purpose the library as a
> storehouse and the librarian as custodian are not enough.[1]

The late library visionary Hugh Atkinson once remarked that an undergraduate library should not be a miniature research library set apart only by the fact that the librarians wear T-shirts and blue jeans. Undergraduate librarians have not sported such attire for some time, but Atkinson's sentiment that there should be fundamental differences between undergraduate and research library services remains true. Undergraduate services modeled on the traditional academic library are inherently ineffective, unresponsive to the information needs of students, and programmatically redundant. This chapter discusses the tension between the traditional libraries and undergraduates, addresses factors that demand a rethinking of undergraduate libraries and services, and defines and presents the gateway library as a model for undergraduate services.

The Tension between Research Libraries and Undergraduates
The academic library, especially the large and complex research library, can be a hostile environment for undergraduates. Historically, the re-

search library was organized and arranged to meet the needs of the humanistic scholar. It served well scholars in disciplines such as English and history who sought that precise sliver of information, that particular edition, that specific translation. The quality of research libraries has traditionally been measured by both total volume count and unique collections. Academic librarians have focused their energy on collection development, the fine points of descriptive cataloging, and the acquisition of sophisticated bibliographic tools that serve the humanist but often do not meet undergraduate needs.

Undergraduates usually do not seek a precise or unique item, but more often just relevant information on a topic. Student interests are seldom as refined as those of the scholar, except when they seek specific titles on course reading lists. To the undergraduate student, books and journal articles are often interchangeable information units.[2] The undergraduate approaches the library with a general subject need unlike the scholar seeking a specific publication. The undergraduate is not well served by the library full of the esoteric, but lacking sufficient material on popular or assigned topics.

The subject-based organization of research libraries can also stymie undergraduates who come with interdisciplinary research interests. The student listens to the public relations rhetoric concerning the richness of the collection but then becomes frustrated when he or she has to spend seemingly endless hours searching through complex and daunting library book stacks or traveling to numerous branch libraries to gather sources that may or may not meet his or her needs. This kind of library is not a general library, the kind of library many students would prefer.

The response of academic libraries is too slow for undergraduate research needs. To the student, deadlines are inflexible, out of their control, and subsequently stressful. A failing grade is the penalty for not getting the sources needed by the paper's due date. A student may be assigned as many as ten library research papers in a sixteen-week semester. Even the most disciplined student with excellent time management skills can devote only a couple of weeks to the research. Unlike the scholar, the student is not able to wait two weeks for interlibrary loan to deliver or even two days for items to be retrieved from remote storage.

Traditionally, research libraries do not provide the kind and quantity of space students require. When surveyed, students express a desire for libraries that provide comfortable study areas, space for group discussion, places to spread out their materials and to leave them when they go off to classes or dinner, and quiet study zones.[3]

In contrasting undergraduate and faculty library use, David C. Taylor points out that undergraduates need background information on broad subjects, require a few relevant citations, use a few indexes and periodicals heavily, compete with one another for the same materials, are unaware of the basic literature on a subject, work under the constraints of short and competing deadlines, and are "other-directed." The faculty member needs information in narrow specialized subjects, requires the right citation, browses in several relevant journals often relying on citation searching, has a specialist's knowledge of relevant literature, works under self-imposed deadlines, and is self-directed.[4] Barbara Valentine studied whether undergraduates, in fact, have a view of research that is different from that of librarians and faculty.[5] The dominant theme to emerge from the focus groups she conducted was that students sought the easiest, least painful way to complete a research project in a timely and satisfactory fashion. For many students, conducting "easy" research meant starting with something familiar. She also found that interactions with peers had a great influence on which sources were selected and to what degree they were used.

Because undergraduate needs are different from those of faculty and scholars, students have traditionally not been well served by research libraries organized, funded, and staffed to respond to the requirements of researchers. In an attempt to better serve undergraduates, many universities have established undergraduate libraries within the context of the larger research library.

The Evolving Undergraduate Library
Although this section of the paper treats the development of the undergraduate library as an autonomous and separate facility, some undergraduate libraries have disappeared over the years, others have been reshaped, and still others have been built anew. In this paper, the undergraduate library as a separate facility serves as a metaphor for library service specially designed for undergraduates.

The undergraduate library movement resulted from librarians and campus administrators acknowledging that research libraries were not designed to respond to the special, particularly space, needs of students. Keyes D. Metcalf wrote in 1949 that the three premises of Harvard's prototype undergraduate library were:

1. that undergraduates will make more and better use of a library designed expressly for them;
2. that this was the best way to relieve the pressure in the Widener building (the research library) and make unnecessary a new central library building;
3. that if that pressure were relieved, the Widener Library building would become a more satisfactory research center than it has been in the past.[6]

Metcalf underscored space as a primary motive in the early development of undergraduate libraries.

As more universities followed Harvard's lead in establishing a distinct library for undergraduates, the impetus to do so shifted from space considerations to developing appropriate, accessible collections. When Irene Braden (later Hoadley) published her review of undergraduate libraries in 1970, she outlined six purposes:[7]

1. providing open access to the collection to avoid the difficulties of the closed stack system;
2. centralizing and simplifying services to the undergraduate;
3. providing a collection of carefully selected books containing the titles all undergraduates should be exposed to for their liberal education, as well as incorporating the reserved-book collection;
4. attempting to make the library an instructional tool by planning it as a center for instruction in library use, to prepare undergraduates for using larger collections, and by staffing it with librarians interested in teaching the undergraduate the resources of a library and the means of tapping those resources;
5. providing services additional to those given by the research collection;
6. constructing a building with the undergraduate's habits of use in mind.

More recently, Roland C. Person argued that the most successful undergraduate libraries are those that have moved beyond being study facilities and book collections.[8] The best undergraduate libraries are those that have become partners in the educational mission of the university. Carla Stoffle underscores this finding:

> In sum, these libraries were created to be outreach oriented and proactive in approach, focusing on students and operating under the assumption that the library had its own role in the education of the undergraduate.[9]

The successful undergraduate libraries enjoy a special status on university campuses. They have become a symbol of commitment to undergraduate education, pointed to with pride by administrators, faculty, librarians, and students. The undergraduate library is included on campus tours to prospective students, concerned parents, and visiting scholars. Promotional videos illustrate the university's commitment to students by highlighting the "Undergrad." Alumni stop by to visit the library where they studied and socialized. Student and alumni groups raise money for the undergraduate library because of its symbolic centrality to undergraduate education. Library administrators cheerfully give grants to the undergraduate library because of its high visibility on campus. The successful undergraduate library is an integral part of the academic and personal lives of students. The sheer number of undergraduates who pass through the turnstiles daily attest to the importance of the place. Students choose to film broadcasting assignments, hold homecoming balloting, distribute newspapers, play initiation pranks, and leave messages for their friends in the Undergrad. As Nina Miley, a former student at the University of Illinois at Urbana-Champaign, remembers:

> For the Undergrad I shall remember the incredible range of activities that went on there. The films, the clever viewing booths, the computer lab always swamped, the magazine collection devoured, the browsing area full of reading, sleeping, talking students. Some people will tell you, with

that certain tone of voice, that the Undergrad is just a bar without beer. I'd take that as a compliment.[10]

Undergraduate libraries fill genuine educational, social, personal, and symbolic needs of students, alumni, administrators, and faculty.

Rethinking the Undergraduate Library[11]

Although undergraduate libraries have achieved special status on more than thirty U. S. and Canadian campuses, profound changes in demographics, information technology, educational mandates, and an information-based society demand a rethinking of undergraduate library services. The undergraduate library established in the 1940s, expanded in the 1950s, and redesigned in the 1970s does not fulfill the needs of students in the 1990s.

Changing Demographics

Of all the transitions taking place concurrently during the past decade, none is more important than the dramatic shifts in the composition of the nation's population. For those involved in higher education, these shifts are reflected in the decline of the traditional college-age population (eighteen to twenty-four years old); a concomitant increase in older, part-time, and adult students; increased commitment to enrollment of minority students; and the influx of international students to universities and colleges.

Decreasing Traditional College Age Pool. In 1986, the baby boom's impact on higher education fizzled. As the boomers graduated, new students known as the baby busters arrived. According to Charles Anderson, the traditional college-age population stood at twenty-eight million in 1986; four years later this group decreased to twenty-six million.[12]

Demographers warned university admission officers that the shrinking pool would result in decreased college enrollments and ultimately, the closing of some institutions. University administrators responded by targeting individuals outside the traditional age pool—older students. Anderson points out that in 1985, of the 12.2 million college students, 5.1 million, or 42 percent, were twenty-five years of age or older, a 24 percent increase in the number of that group attending college compared to ten years earlier. By 1995, their ranks had grown to 6.2 million, roughly 44 percent of all students.[13] These new students came to higher education with different experiences, motivations, learning styles, educational demands, personal · obligations, and financial situations.

The four-year baccalaureate became less and less common because of the growing number of students who attended school part-time while holding down a job or balancing family obligations. In 1970, about 68 percent of all students attended college full-time whereas the remaining 32 percent attended on a part-time basis. In 1980, the percentages were 59 percent full-time and 41 percent part-time; in 1994, 57 and 43 percent respectively.[14]

Minority Enrollments. During the 1980s, colleges and universities mounted minority recruitment and retention programs as a response to population shifts, federal mandates, and a desire to move toward a multicultural university.

U.S. population growth is at a historic low. The overall fertility rate in the United States has been on a downward trend for the past twenty years. Leobardo Estrada points out that minority groups represent an exception to the overall pattern of decline with a growth rate of two to fourteen times greater than those for the nonminority population.[15] However, despite growing minority populations, minority students are not represented proportionally in higher education enrollments. Although the percentage of African-American students graduating from high school increased about 20 percent in the years between the 1970s and the 1990s, the percentage attending college was 25 percent less than that of white students. A similar disparity exists for Hispanics.[16]

Administrative and federal mandates for the recruitment and retention of increasing numbers of minority students have their historical basis in the educational and social upheaval of the 1960s. Universities and colleges began setting up programs to target, matriculate, and graduate students who had historically been excluded from higher education. Some universities have been successful in increasing the numbers of minority students. In 1980, 9.1 percent of college students were African-American, and by 1990, the number had increased to 11.3 percent.[17] However, by the mid 1990s, public support for affirmative action had declined. In California, for example , citizens approved Proposition 209, a measure outlawing racial preference in public employment, education, and contracting. The immediate result was a decline in minority enrollment in California. Legal action has also been taken in other states to limit affirmative action.[18] As a result some states are changing their admission requirements to eliminate racial biases.[19] However, without these corrective measures, if the trend to eliminate affirmative action continues, the consequences for the nation and for higher education will be dramatically negative. The economic as well as the social fabric of the country is dependent on how successful the larger society and institutions of higher education are in encouraging full participation for all citizens, particularly minority citizens.[20]

International Students. Over the past decade, international students have had an increased presence on university campuses and in academic libraries. Marianthi Zikopoulos's report documents that in the year 1980, 311,882 international students were enrolled at colleges and universities in the United States. In 1992–1993, this number had gone up to 438,618.[21] Indeed, beginning with post–World War II initiatives to open the doors to American universities, the number of international students enrolled has increased over one hundredfold.

An American education is a desirable commodity especially for students from those nations whose educational systems, research facilities, and technological knowledge are not as evolved or as readily available. Given the desirability and relative affordability of an American education, coupled with governmental and institutional financial incentives, it is not surprising that international students have filled the classes left vacant by the baby bust.

Zikopoulos's data show that in addition to the significant increase in the numbers of international students, shifts have occurred in the country of origin. Two changes stand out: the greatly increased percentage of students coming from Asia, and the decreased percentage of students from the Middle East. Zikopoulos points out that at some universities and colleges, international students represent a greater percentage of the student body than even the overall minority student enrollment in the United States.

Information Technology

Today's undergraduates represent the first generation raised in Alvin Toffler's electronic cottage, with its microcomputers, videocassette recorders (VCRs), car phones, modems, faxes, gameboys, and walkmans.[22] According to the *Statistical Abstract of the United States 1997*, in 1984–1985, there were 631,983 computers in elementary and secondary education: by 1996–1997, these schools had 6,854,026. Likewise in 1994, 35 percent of K–12 schools had Internet access. That jumped to 65 percent in 1996.[23] In 1980, 1.1 percent of American households had a VCR;[24] in 1993, the percentage skyrocketed to 77.1 percent.[25] This accelerated change in the use and availability of technology has altered students' expectations of libraries. Unlike students of the past, most students today view information technologies as laborsaving devices—tools to be exploited rather than feared.

When undergraduate libraries first established media centers in the late 1970s, slides and audiotapes were considered non-traditional acquisitions for libraries. Since then, media and information technologies have converged, offering unprecedented opportunities for information storage, instruction, and creation. These new formats are now commonplace in library collections. Multimedia systems, a technology that supports both active and personalized learning as well as nonlinear information retrieval, are already in widespread use. Expert systems, an application of artificial intelligence, have exciting potential for teaching information evaluation skills "because expert systems can simulate the problem-solving processes of an expert."[26]

Macro trends in computer and communication technology point to increasing use of campus, regional, national, and international information networks. Libraries are building expanded catalogs with interfaces (software designed to guide the user in the selection and use of multiple databases and options) on increasingly powerful workstations. The revolutionary influence of computerized information dissemination, along with the resultant information overload, have changed how undergraduates locate information. The presence in the library of CD-ROM and locally mounted databases, as well as the growing trend toward resources accessed through the World Wide Web, has greatly increased the student's ability to identify sources of information on a particular subject, but they have also increased the difficulty of choosing the best or most appropriate sources. Also, with the availability of the Web, an expanded computer hardware base, and an ever-increasing number of information resources accessible remotely, many students have become invisible library users.

Educational Mandates

Since the founding of the first undergraduate library, changes in curricula and educational demands have reshaped the undergraduate experience. The years have witnessed an increase in the number of classes using collaborative learning, resource-based teaching, group work, and case studies. Most recently, a number of commissions have called for broad-based educational reform because schools are not educating students either in the basics or in how to function in the modern world. In this changing world, skills and information become dated quickly, making it difficult to know what should be taught. What educators seem to agree on is that students can no longer be expected to master a finite set of skills that will last a lifetime. Education reformers, business leaders, librarians, and futurists have all called for teaching students how to learn so that learning becomes a dynamic, lifelong process. The U.S. National Commission on Excellence in Education called for the creation of a learning society in its report, *A Nation at Risk*:

> At the heart of such a society is the commitment to a set of values and to a system of education that affords all members the opportunity to stretch their minds to full capacity, from early childhood through adulthood, learning more as the world itself changes. Such a society has as a basic foundation the idea that education is important not only because of what it contributes to one's career goals but also because of the value it adds to the general quality of one's life.[27]

In an information society, students feel increased pressure to learn how to learn. In a society in which skills and knowledge are quickly dated, education does not end with a diploma. In such a society, many individuals may have three or four distinct careers during their work life and learning must become a lifelong enterprise. Crucial to lifelong learning is the ability to sort through and evaluate the millions of bits of information bombarding a person from the media, print sources, and conversation. Successful individuals in an information society must make good decisions regarding their consumption of information. Critical, reflective, and reasonable thinking, focused on deciding what to believe or how to act, is an essential intellectual survival skill. In an information society, knowing how to retrieve and evaluate information, as opposed to having physical access to, or ownership of, information is the mark of an educated person.[28] Knowing how to find high-quality information for personal and work use will determine one's success or failure. Students faced with an increasingly complex society need sophisticated information management skills.

Information-based Society

Today's undergraduates are products of an information-based society. Students have grown up in a society where increasing numbers of jobs involve services, communications, and information. Jobs now demand different skills and abilities from those demanded fifteen years ago. Students live in a world in which information increases geometrically and no one person can expect to keep pace with it. Students have seen their parents make career changes, go back to school for retraining after their jobs have become obsolete, and struggle to learn new computer systems. These students know nothing other than the information society.

Undergraduates and the world in which they live have changed dramatically since Metcalf wrote nearly fifty years ago. Given demographic shifts in the undergraduate population, the impact of information technologies, the increasing educational demands of a knowledge-based work force, and the influence of evolving social and economic structures, librarians serving undergraduates must develop innovative and creative responses to these new challenges. These challenges are so profound as to require a rethinking of undergraduate library services and the subsequent development of a new model predicated on the library as gateway.

The Gateway Library

When the first undergraduate library opened in 1949, the library was a space, a place to send the undergraduates, taking pressure off the research facility. As more undergraduate libraries were established, the distinguishing characteristic was the collection. When the University of Illinois dedicated its new undergraduate facility in 1969, the opening-day brochure highlighted the ample study space and the judiciously selected liberal arts collection. No mention was made of reference or instructional services; the library would not establish a reference desk until a decade later. During the late 1970s and 1980s, bibliographic instruction was the defining focus of undergraduate services. Undergraduate libraries initiated instructional partnerships most often with English composition faculty, striving to integrate instruction into the educational framework of the university. Although many undergraduate libraries have enjoyed considerable success in the area of bibliographic instruction, more often than not, the library continues to be viewed by faculty as a support service. The weakness inherent in this support service model is the placement of the library in an adjunct relationship to students and professors. This tenuous position, taken together with changes discussed earlier in this paper in demographics, information technologies, educational mandates, and an information-based society, suggests that the undergraduate library must be reshaped and refocused into something quite different—a gateway library.

The gateway library, unlike the old undergraduate library, is not defined by physical space, collection, or library-initiated services. The Gateway Arch in St. Louis symbolizes westward movement as Easterners traveled to a promised land, stopping on the shores of the Mississippi, surveying their options, purchasing provisions, and joining up with trail scouts. Metaphorically, the gateway library performs the same functions. As a gateway, the undergraduate library is a threshold to the information world beyond, providing linkages with subject-based collections, specialized library services, computer networks, instructional opportunities throughout campus, and electronic information sources.[29] The library serves as the entry point for the undergraduate, the beginning researcher, and the technologically uninitiated. The gateway library is not defined by physical space or a discrete collection but, rather, by linkages to information sources and learning opportunities beyond the library's walls and by access enhanced through technology.

The gateway library is a direct outgrowth of information technologies. Academic libraries have leveraged technology to expedite resource sharing through electronic networks and document delivery, acknowledging that no one institution can afford to own every item needed by its local academic community. Online authority control has decentralized bibliographic processing, hastening the end of the central cataloging department once required by proximity to a manual headings file. Reference librarians are questioning whether traditional desk service is viable or appropriate as more and more individuals gain access to the library remotely. Reference service defined by a desk and proscribed hours reflects a time when one had to physically enter the library to find information. The gateway library is predicated on a wall-less library, information access being as important as ownership, and the value of programmatically linking technologists, educators, librarians, and students. The gateway library has six defining elements: (1) innovative use of technology; (2) programmatic partnerships; (3) a laboratory environment; (4) an educational framework; (5) inclusiveness; and (6) user-centered advocacy.[30]

Innovative Use of Technology

Over the past decade, technology has revolutionized the look and feel of the nation's libraries. Even the most clairvoyant librarian could not have envisioned the rapid development and broad-based availability of dynamic information technologies evident in academic libraries. A few years ago, CD-ROM and Gophers were hot, new technologies, but now the Web has supplanted them. The gateway library addresses the transitory nature of developing technologies. Its emphasis is on training and use of technology in general rather than on the use of particular technologies.

The gateway library is both a technology showplace and a laboratory. The newest technologies and software releases are made available for the campus community to test, manipulate, and explore. New technologies presented in a nonprescriptive manner and unrestricted experimentation is the norm. The gateway library is the testing ground for new equipment and applications. In the laboratory atmosphere of the gateway, students become the test pilots of multimedia, expert systems, and adaptive technology.

In the gateway library, students have access to a full range of information technologies, including supercatalogs, CD-ROM, interactive video, virtual reality systems, imaging hardware, touch screens, full-text databases, and emerging technology and systems. However, the gateway library does not present technology for technology's sake but, rather, for its potential to enhance student access, learning, and research. As Patricia Glass Schuman writes: "Workstations—or any technology, for that matter—are a means for extending the capacity of the human brain. They do not replace it."[31] Technology in the gateway library should be used to expand the world and enlarge the capabilities of students.

Programmatic Partnerships
Just as academic libraries have learned that collections are interdependent, so too have undergraduate librarians realized that they cannot provide effective services without collaboration with other educators and campus offices. No undergraduate library can provide single-handedly all the expertise, resources, or innovative ideas needed in the gateway library. Mutual cooperation and shared visions are fundamental to programmatic partnerships among undergraduate libraries, computing centers, academic departments, academic support services, development offices, and university administration.

The Undergraduate Library at the University of Illinois at Urbana-Champaign serves as a case study in successful cooperative partnerships. Illinois librarians recognized that efforts needed to be programmatic, not designed as support services, if the Undergraduate Library were to be an integral element in the academic life of students. They aggressively forged strategic partnerships with individuals and offices that shared responsibility for undergraduate education. The appendix to this chapter describes Illinois's cooperative initiatives that illustrate the concrete outcomes of programmatic partnerships.

At the University of Washington, librarians have collaborated with a broad range of other campus professionals to address the challenge of bringing technology into the service of teaching and learning, the new information literacy, and the creation of community at a large research university. This collaboration has resulted in UWired, a holistic, campuswide approach to creating an electronic community in which communication, collaboration, and information technologies become ongoing, integral parts of teaching and learning. UWired is a collaboration of faculty, librarians, computing staff, administrators, and students from a number of units, including Undergraduate Education, Computing & Communications, University Libraries, and University Extension. UWired addresses faculty development, active and engaged student learning, and facilities management and redesign. Few efforts elsewhere have brought to bear such diverse expertise and support to enhance campuswide learning and teaching. Although initiatives on other campuses have provided computers to faculty or students, UWired goes beyond technology—offering sustained discipline-specific instruction, useful applications of technology in the classroom, faculty development, and requisite facilities and infrastructure. Early in the evolution of UWired, librarians were recognized as key players in the enterprise. The librarians provided the intellectual framework for placing technology in its proper place as an enabling tool for the new information literacy.[32]

Programmatic partnerships demand several key skills and attitudes on the part of librarians. Librarians need to be able to articulate the mission of the gateway clearly and point out mutual benefits to all partners. They must seize opportunities unhesitatingly when a partnership proposal comes along. Institutional and personal tolerance for shared control is essential to collaboration. The pitfalls to programmatic partnerships are the potential for conflicts in purposes, new training needs, and loss of total control. However, the advantages outweigh the negatives. The spiraling demands on information providers and educators require that partnerships be nurtured in the gateway library. As Cliff Bishop writes:

Where drawbacks are suitably noted and controlled, however, the advantages of cooperation are significant. Programs and services are enhanced. Additional and different expertise can be acquired. Staff is augmented. Campus services are able to extend their hours and improve their outreach.[33]

Thus, programmatic partnerships, a keystone of the gateway library, are solidified.

Laboratory Environment

The undergraduate library as gateway library is by its very nature a laboratory. As a laboratory, the library creates an environment where new approaches and structures are encouraged, innovation and risk-taking rewarded, and user behavior and needs studied continuously. Given the dynamic nature of information technology and the changing needs of the gateway's clientele, creative approaches and fluid organizational structures are paramount. Traditional organizational structures defined by function or departmental affiliation will not work in the gateway library. The best environment for creative work is modeled on the extended family where people get to know each other and find autonomy within a larger whole. A group could be composed of individuals with a common interest in the project, pilot, or new approach. For instance, a working group of librarians and computer programmers with individual expertise and experience in user education, database design, relevant subject expertise, staff training, and programming could be gathered to guide the development and implementation of super-catalog access to *PsycINFO*. It is not the individual intelligence that is important, but the group's IQ. When the work is completed, the group would disband and go on to the next project. In the gateway library, the structure must allow for project development, foster interdepartmental collaboration, create a safe haven for ideas, and link program needs with expertise whether or not it is found in the library.

The University of Washington's UWired collaboration is predicated on such a model. UWired is organized into work groups made up of faculty, librarians, and computing staff that represent a number of campus units. These work groups have overseen the construction of three "collaboratories," resolving hardware and software issues for the ongoing program; refining the freshmen seminar curriculum; implementing an upper-division program; developing distance-learning courses; designing a faculty development lab; and creating new models for ongoing faculty training.

Innovation requires an organizational climate in which risk-taking and creativity are encouraged and rewarded. Stagnation results when risk-taking and the inevitable failures are punished. The staff members of the gateway library need to encourage each other to try new approaches, share ideas, and trust each other. Administrators need to publicly applaud and reward individuals who take risks and encourage people to be open to change. As Larry Wilson of the Pecos River Learning Center says, "You'll always do what you've always done if you always think the way you've always thought."[34] It is only through constant experimentation that a tradition of creativity emerges.

A mission of the gateway library is to study user behavior and the most effective way to provide links between students and information. Pilot projects can evaluate new methods, products, and coalitions without causing major disruptions to proven operations or a drain on the library's resources. Historically, undergraduate students have been receptive to experimental programs and are not yet mired in tradition or hindered by hardened research habits. The library can become a research lab in which to study student behavior, socioeconomic factors influencing library use, and the impact of technology. Katina Strauch emphasizes the fundamental responsibility of librarians to carry out research:

> To affect our world, however, we must be prepared to be active participants. Research is one approach to influencing the world of information and knowledge. We practitioners must believe that what we do is important enough to warrant examination and study. We must be prepared to study the long-range or amorphous issues as well as the functionary concerns of day-to-day operations. And all of us—library directors, library educators, and practicing librarians—must buy into this. Research in our profession

is not gratuitous; on the contrary, good research is badly
needed. [35]

The gateway library provides an ideal environment in which to carry
out that research.

Educational Framework
The gateway library is a teaching facility more than a book warehouse
or study hall. All services, programs, and resource decisions must be
evaluated in terms of how they enhance and support the gateway library's
commitment to the underlying educational mission of the college or
university. Philip Tompkins suggests that framing decisions in how
learning is enhanced reconceptualizes the library:

> This opportunity to rethink the role of the library in
> support of learning derives from the convergence of five
> factors: (1) a newly aligned influential group of computer-
> literate students, teachers, librarians, computer profession-
> als, media specialists, planners, and architects who are
> beginning to transcend their traditionally separate
> cultures; (2) the seeding of any and every building on
> campus with microcomputer technologies; (3) a growing
> sense of legitimacy and importance of student learning
> wherever it may occur on (and off) campuses; (4) a
> consensus about the need to create campus environments
> that are by design productive for teaching and learning;
> and (5) the current availability of resources to program,
> design, and construct (or renovate and expand) libraries
> supportive of the reform of undergraduate teaching and
> learning.[36]

The educational framework of the gateway library finds
antecedents in the bibliographic instruction programs pioneered in
undergraduate libraries. From its early focus on library orientation,
bibliographic instruction has moved along a continuum that has been
influenced by changing users, evolving library environments, and an
increased understanding of how individuals learn. Perhaps one of the

most significant developments of the 1970's and 1980's was the shift away from tool-based to concept-based instruction. For example, David F. Kohl and Lizabeth A. Wilson found that users learned transferable information skills more readily when using conceptual frameworks and a cognitive approach to research skills instruction.[37] Their study compared the effect of two approaches to instruction on students' use of information sources. The control group was taught a traditional tool-specific approach to information-seeking, characterized by the introduction of a generic, prescriptive research strategy. Students were instructed on searching some of the key tools (such as catalogs, indexes and abstracts, and bibliographies). The experimental group was taught a cognitive approach to information-seeking in which the research strategy was adapted to fit the structure of the relevant literature. Students in this pilot group were encouraged to begin with research questions and to identify relevant tools based on the corresponding discipline's literature. Kohl and Wilson compared and scored the two groups' bibliographies on a set of criteria. The scores assigned to the bibliographies of the students taught a cognitive approach were significantly higher than scores assigned to the bibliographies of the students in the control group. Besides producing better results on classroom assignments, concept-based learning provides new information literacy skills needed for lifelong learning.

In the gateway library, undergraduates will confront on-line systems with the likes of periodical indices, locally developed databases, and electronic bulletin boards. Will students embrace such a machine blindly, walk away overwhelmed, avoid it altogether, or understand its scope and limitations? Users need critical thinking skills in order to cope with the overwhelming information choices. Increasingly, librarians will partner with faculty in teaching students how to make informed decisions in the information-intense environment of the gateway library. To teach critical thinking, librarians will use active and personalized learning techniques that are effective in teaching these higher-level cognitive skills.

Active learning demands that students participate in the process of learning by doing, not passively listening to a library lecture. Students are given more autonomy and power over choice in active learning environments. Active learning that shifts the responsibility for learning from the instructor to the individual can stimulate abstract thinking, the essence of critical evaluation.

Personalized learning is based on the belief that students are heterogeneous and that their differences are to be recognized and embraced. As Arthur W. Combs wrote:

> For 150 years we have been trying to teach students as though they were alike. We have grouped them, tracked them, grade-leveled them, and tried to homogenize and organize them into one kind of group or another for administrative expedience.[38]

Personalized education emphasizes learning goals according to individual abilities and without artificial time schedules. Because the library and information skills of the entering undergraduates vary widely, personalized learning is crucial.

Even though not all emerging educational technologies will live up to their press releases, the gateway library will increasingly exploit these technologies. Educational technology at its best will enhance the communication of information and understanding in the learning process. Already in development and widespread use is multimedia, a technology that promotes both active and personalized learning. Development of nonlinear software such as hypertext and Web browsers has enabled librarians to author computer-assisted instruction packages not possible with earlier software, and such systems hold promise in the teaching of information evaluation skills.

In the gateway library, librarians, in collaboration with faculty, computing professionals, and students, will teach the critical thinking skills that enable students to succeed in a world of information overload and will use active learning, personalized learning, and educational technology to enhance undergraduate education.

Inclusiveness

The gateway library is a place in which all students, regardless of background or experience, are comfortable pursuing their information needs. A major impetus for rethinking undergraduate services is the increasingly pluralistic student body. The gateway library embraces that diversity through its staff, its programs, and its priorities.

The staff of the gateway library is heterogeneous—from student employees to clerks to librarians. Individuals of diverse backgrounds should be actively recruited in the new undergraduate library, starting with student assistants. Undergraduates are the harbingers of change in higher education; minorities are represented in greater percentages in the undergraduate population than graduate or faculty ranks. One way to recruit minorities to librarianship is to encourage student assistants to consider librarianship. A diverse staff must be trained to be sensitive to each other as well as to student cultures and learning styles. The gateway library celebrates the variety and richness of a diverse staff.

The gateway library accommodates the different learning styles of a heterogeneous user population. In a multicultural student population, instruction practitioners will be teaching classrooms of diverse learners. Diversity of learners is not new in libraries, but librarians have only recently acknowledged and responded to learners as a heterogeneous population. As the heterogeneous student body with diverse learning styles becomes increasingly pluralistic, there will be a need for even greater sensitivity in the selection of teaching styles.

Most important, the gateway library provides an environment in which individual contributions and vision are highly valued. The quality of programs and initiatives in the gateway library is a direct outgrowth of the commitment of its staff. Each person has a unique role to play. As Hugh Atkinson was fond of saying, success is not a zero sum game. There is room for everyone to succeed and reach levels of excellence. An environment that allows each person to contribute his or her best, that welcomes diversity of experience and opinion, and that values individual integrity and input is a requirement for the success of the gateway library.

User-centered Advocacy

User-centered advocacy is key to a gateway library in which high-quality services and user satisfaction are goals recognized and shared by all library staff.[39] Because the gateway model is so different from academic library traditions, the gateway librarian must advocate for students in the library, on campus, and beyond the profession. Ultimately, the gateway librarian should provide opportunities for students to become their own advocates.

Advocacy within the Library. As with any librarian serving a defined clientele, the undergraduate librarian serves as their advocate in the library, making the case for appropriate resources, policies and procedures, services and staff. Undergraduate librarians articulate how the library as an institution can respond to the unique needs of undergraduates.

Because undergraduate services typically support the largest group of users, the financial demands of an undergraduate library, though proportionate to the number of patrons served, often tend to overshadow the funding needs of smaller units. Unless the undergraduate librarian successfully presents the case of undergraduates to colleagues and administrators, the gateway library will be seen as an adversary. Tompkins explains that budgets and funding for the gateway library are fundamentally different from those for a traditional academic library:

> Finally, the budget for such a facility will reflect different priorities than those of a typical university library budget, built on the classic model of print technology adjusted by the demands of library and campus information systems. The point being made here is that besides the need for restructuring the budgets of the research library, there is a need for a new and separate budget constructed for the teaching library that reflects a fledgling effort to develop a collaborative institution on campus, cultivating an ethos springing from the requirements of teaching and learning in a technology-intensive environment.[40]

Campus Advocate. The undergraduate librarian is equally obliged to serve as the student's advocate on campus. As undergraduate advocates, they need to be leaders in university committees, governing bodies, and curriculum committees, and collaborators with teaching faculty, building the partnerships necessary in the gateway library. Undergraduate librarians offer campus administrators an unusual perspective. They are in the position to provide a broad understanding of the needs, fears, and frustrations of students. Any librarian working the reference desk or teaching a session can easily key into students' pressing personal and academic strains. Undergraduate students write papers on suicide, stress, anorexia nervosa, steroid use, or AIDS because these topics are of immediate concern to them. Students perceive the library as nonthreatening and one of the few places they can get individualized help. For this reason, they express their concerns readily and often through the open avenue of the reference interview. The humanizing knowledge gained in these interviews can be given to the administration to help it improve campus life for students.

Advocate in the Profession The undergraduate librarian must also serve as the student's advocate in the profession. As a special interest group, the Undergraduate Librarians Discussion Group of the Association of College and Research Libraries, undergraduate librarians issue guidelines, standards, and publications; hold programs and conferences; influence vendors and publishers; and convey concerns to the greater library community. Undergraduate librarians especially need to contact vendors and publishers, serving as the students' advocate to influence the development and refinement of information technologies used in the gateway library. Through committee liaisons, user groups, and personal contacts, undergraduate librarians can make the needs of the undergraduate student known to producers of information technologies.

Advocacy beyond the Profession. Undergraduate librarians need to reach out beyond their own field and become involved in organizations and associations focused on undergraduate education (e.g., American Association of Higher Education, National Council of Teachers of English). By joining these groups, attending their conferences, presenting papers, and serving on panels, librarians can inform others about the library as gateway, gathering support and understanding for the educational role of libraries. By actively collaborating in research and publication endeavors with counterpart organizations, the scope of advocacy broadens beyond specific institutions.

Students as Advocates. Ideally, students should speak for themselves and become their own advocates. Librarians need to strengthen the user-centered library, to build the student's personal identification with the library, and in essence, to make the gateway library the undergraduate's library of choice. Undergraduate librarians need to involve students in the library by appointing undergraduates to library committees and advisory bodies, and by providing mechanisms for suggestions and complaints through the traditional suggestion box, the flashier question board, or an electronic mail box.[41] User surveys and focus group interviews need to be considered a routine component of planning in the gateway library. Undergraduate libraries can encourage student investment and advocacy through relatively simple steps. Proven means include suggesting that honor societies contribute money to buy books in the name of outstanding students, offering display cases and space for student causes and exhibits, and approaching instructors to offer library problems for students to study and solve.

Undergraduate librarians need to become involved in student concerns and life. They can volunteer to serve as advisors for student organizations such as fraternities, sororities, student government, cultural clubs, and international student organizations. There are numerous opportunities for informal exchanges with students at residence hall dinners, departmental lectures, and college receptions.

All librarians must embrace their role as the student's advocate. They must present the needs of students clearly to library colleagues and administrators and lobby for necessary resources. Gateway librarians must participate actively in the establishment of campus priorities, services, and educational goals. Likewise, they need to increase their visibility as advocates within the library profession. Undergraduate librarians should seize the opportunity to play the advocacy role outside the field to others involved in undergraduate education. Perhaps most important, through involving students in the library, librarians can encourage students to serve as their own advocates when they move beyond the gateway.

Conclusion
Hugh Atkinson was right. The undergraduate library should respond to the needs of students by more than informal attire. Since the estab-

lishment of the first undergraduate library in 1949, the undergraduate library has evolved from a study hall to a collection to a student-centered entity. The profound changes in the nation's demographics, burgeoning information technologies, educational mandates, and an information-based society have stimulated a reexamination of undergraduate library services. It is no longer sufficient to offer nontraditional services. The undergraduate library cannot be defined by space, collections, or personnel but, rather, by services that link students with information and provide the requisite education to manage that information. The undergraduate library becomes a gateway through which students enter, experiment with emerging new technologies, learn critical use of information, connect to information providers, and emerge as self-sufficient information managers. The gateway library is predicated on innovative use of technology, programmatic partnerships with campus educators, creation of a laboratory environment, library functions framed within the context of learning, an atmosphere that values diversity, and user-centered advocacy by librarians. In the gateway library, librarians need not wear T-shirts and blue jeans to distinguish themselves from the research library as Hugh Atkinson suggested because the gateway library is fundamentally distinct in its responsiveness to student needs, programs, and changes not yet anticipated.

Notes

1. Jesse Shera, "Staffing Library Services to Meet Student Needs," in *Libraries and the Organization of Knowledge* (Hamden, Conn.: Archon Bks., 1965), 201.

2. David C. Taylor, "Undergraduates' Use of Periodicals—Implications for Library Reference Work, *Reference Librarian* no. 27/28 (1989): 51–65.

3. Tony Mays, "Do Undergraduates Need Their Libraries?" *Australian Academic and Research Libraries* 17 (June 1986): 59–60.

4. Taylor, "Undergraduates' Use of Periodicals," 58–60.

5. Barbara Valentine, "Undergraduate Research Behavior: Using Focus Groups to Generate Theory," *Journal of Academic Librarianship* 19 (1993): 300–304.

6. Keyes D. Metcalf, "Harvard Faces Its Library Problems," *Harvard Library Bulletin* 3 (spring 1949): 187.

7. Irene Braden, *The Undergraduate Library,* ACRL Monograph no. 31 (Chicago: ALA, 1970), 2.

8. Roland Conrad Person, *A New Path: Undergraduate Libraries at United States and Canadian Universities, 1949–1987* (New York: Greenwood Pr., 1988).

9. Carla Stoffle, "A New Library for the New Undergraduate," *Library Journal* 115 (Oct., 1990): 48.

10. Mary Jane Petrowski and Betsy Wilson, *Research Guide: Introduction to Library and Information Skills* (Champaign: Ill.: Stipes, 1993), 17.

11. Much of this section is based on the author's "Changing Users: Bibliographic Instruction for Whom?" in *The Evolving Educational Mission of the Library*, ed. Betsy Baker and Mary Ellen Litzinger (Chicago: ACRL, 1992), 20–53.

12. Charles Anderson et al., comps., *Fact Book on Higher Education (1989– 1990)* (New York: American Council on Higher Education and Macmillan Publishing Co., 1990), 3.

13. National Center for Education Statistics, *Digest of Education Statistics 1997* (Washington, D.C.: U.S. Department of Education, 1998), 186.

14. Ibid., 182.

15. Leobardo Estrada, "Anticipating the Demographic Future," *Change 20* (May/June 1988): 14.

16. "Part 2. Affirmative Action: History and Rationale" *Affirmative Action Review: Report to the President.* N.p.:n.p., n.d. Online. Available: http:// www.whitehouse.gov/WH/EOP/OP/html/aa/aa02.html.

17. Ibid.

18. William A. Galston, "An Affirmative Action Status Report: Evidence and Options," *Philosophy and Public Policy* 17 (spring 1997): 2–9.

19. Loni Guinier, "An Equal Change," *New York Times*, Apr. 23, 1998, editorial section

20. Stoffle, "A New Library for the New Undergraduate," 48.

21. Marianthi Zikopoulos, ed., *Open Doors 1992/93: Report on International Educational Exchange* (New York: Institute of International Education, 1993), 11.

22. Alvin Toffler, *The Third Wave* (New York: Bantam Bks., 1981).

23. *Statistical Abstract of the United States 1997* (Washington, D.C.: Government Printing Office, 1997), 171.

24. *Statistical Abstract of the United States 1989* (Washington, D.C.: Government Printing Office, 1989), 544 .

25. *Statistical Abstract of the United States 1994* (Washington, D.C.: Government Printing Office, 1994), 567.

26. Valerie Jackson Feinman, "Computers and Library Instruction: Expert Systems," *Computers in Libraries 13* (Mar. 1993): 53.

27. U.S. National Commission on Excellence in Education, *A Nation at Risk: the Imperative for Educational Reform: A Report to the Nation and the Secretary of Education* (Washington, D.C.: Government Printing Office, 1983).

28. American Library Association Presidential Committee on Information Literacy, *Final Report* (Chicago: ALA, 1989).

29. Some of the concepts presented in this paper find parallel development in how the University of Southern California Leavey Library is being defined and shaped. In an interview published in the *USC Chronicle* (Oct. 18, 1993: 4), Peter Lyman states: "The Leavey is intended to be a 'gateway' library. Historically, undergraduate libraries have been study halls and have tried to present a microcosm of knowledge, so that an undergraduate could answer any question they might have in that one place. We think that's fundamentally wrong, that knowledge is so open-ended that no small collection can really represent any field. We don't intend to answer every question."

30. The Leavey Library at the University of Southern California and the concepts being explored at Harvard College Library provide variations on a working model for a gateway library. The mission statement of the Leavey Library describes one definition of the gateway library: "The mission of the Leavey Library is to provide a gateway to library and information resources which support and enrich the undergraduate and graduate curriculum. Specific goals of the program: twenty-four hour access to course reserves and study space; access to basic collections, which support primary course related research; training and consulting services to develop library research skills utilizing both print and digital formats; facilities for faculty, librarians, and students to collaborate in learning and research activities; support for faculty in locating and developing instructional materials." (Oct. 13, 1992). In a discussion paper titled "Gateways to Knowledge: A New Direction for the Harvard College" developed for the Gateways to Knowledge Conference sponsored by the Harvard College Library, November 5–6, 1993, Lawrence Dowler offers a conceptual framework for the gateway library: "Gateway is a metaphor for access to knowledge and evokes the image of crossing a threshold and entering a dramatically expanding world of information and learning; the Library, as gateway, is the means by which students and faculty will locate and use this information. The gateway we envision is the constellation of services, the or-

ganization required for providing these services, and the spaces dedicated to student learning" (page 4).

31. Patricia Glass Schuman, "Reclaiming Our Technological Future," *Library Journal* 115 (Mar., 1990): 37.

32. For more information on the UWired collaboration, consult the program's Web home page available at http://www.washington.edu/uwired.

33. Cliff Bishop et al., "Front and Center: Library Initiatives for Improvement in Undergraduate Education," in *Academic Libraries: Achieving Excellence in Higher Education: Proceedings of the Sixth National Conference of the Association of College and Research Libraries, Salt Lake City, Utah, April 12-14, 1992* (Chicago: ACRL, 1992), 408-11.

34. Larry Wilson, as quoted in Daniel Goleman, Paul Kaufman, and Michael Ray, *The Creative Spirit* (New York: Dutton, 1992), 134.

35. Katina Strauch, "The Power of Positive Thinking, *"Journal of Academic Librarianship* 18 (May 1992): 101.

36. Philip Tompkins, "New Structures for Teaching Libraries," *Library Administration and Management* 4 (spring 1990): 77–78.

37. David F. Kohl and Lizabeth A. Wilson, "Effectiveness of Course-Integrated Bibliographic Instruction in Improving Coursework," *RQ 26* (winter 1986): 206–11.

38. Arthur W. Combs, "What the Future Demands of Education," *Phi Delta Kappan 62* (Jan. 1981): 372.

39. For a definition of the user-centered library and the assessment infrastructure needed to move toward and maintain such a library, see Lizabeth A. Wilson, "Building the User-Centered Library, " *RQ 34* (spring 1995): 297-302.

40. Tompkins, "New Structures for Teaching Libraries," 80.

41. Donna Pittman Blomberg, "The Question Board," *College & Research Libraries News* 48 (June 1987): 327–30.

Appendix
Programs and Services Based on Programmatic Partnerships
at the Undergraduate Library, University of Illinois
at Urbana-Champaign.

1. User Education
Illinois has a long-standing commitment to teaching undergraduate students to make full, self-sufficient, and sophisticated use of information resources. The user education program is based on the firm belief that to perform to the best of their abilities in university courses, as well as in independent intellectual inquiry, students must be able to make informed and judicious use of the library and its resources.

The undergraduate librarians, working closely with the teaching faculty, have developed what many consider to be— among those offered at major universities—the preeminent course-integrated bibliographic instruction program in the country. It was first integrated into the curriculum in 1979, and now reaches all freshmen and transfer students enrolled in courses that fulfill the university's rhetoric requirement. Extensive financial support from the university, including three Undergraduate Instructional Awards, has permitted continual development and enhancement of the program. Nine instructional modules have been devised, each designed to address the special instructional needs and educational preparation of the distinct populations that make up the university's diverse student body. Care has also been taken to employ a variety of teaching methods in order to make the program optimally responsive to the variety of learning styles evinced by a student body of such diversity. Fundamental to the success of the program is the educational partnership between librarians and faculty.

2. CD-ROM Site/Periodical Information Desk
The CD-ROM site provides students with access to networked optical disc systems for information retrieval. Staff at the periodical information desk assist students in the selection, use, and evaluation of these databases. Development of the site is a result of a

The descriptions are based on the handout "University of Illinois at Urbana-Champaign Undergraduate Library: Programs and Services" composed by Cliff Bishop and Lizabeth Wilson, March 1992.

financial and technological partnership with the campus's emerging technology board.

3. College and Career Cluster

The College and Career Cluster, begun in 1982, is a special self-service collection of college handbooks, job and career guides, test preparation sources, and college rankings. The cluster also includes a microfiche collection of college catalogs from American as well as selected foreign universities. A recent grant, from the Mothers' and Dads' Associations of the University of Illinois, will permit further expansion and enhancement of the cluster with media materials and computer databases as well as relevant software. Planning for the cluster is a cooperative venture with the professionals in the campus's career development office.

4. Development Efforts

There are a number of continuing cooperative development efforts. Special funding for projects and publicity has been obtained with the assistance of the Development and Public Affairs Office of the University Library. Its annual funds program is undertaken by the Library Friends organization, a special division of which is the Student Friends group. Senior class gifts, in 1988, 1991 and 1992, permitted purchase of the magazine collection (consisting of general-interest periodicals on film cassettes) and extensive renovation and landscaping of the library courtyard. A tuition lottery held in 1990 by the Mothers' and Dads' Associations raised $15,000 toward the improvement of the Career Cluster, and additional grants of $5,000 have been provided in each subsequent year. The Dads' Association also contributes an annual gift to the library, calculated at twenty-five dollars for each sophomore who has maintained a grade point average of 5.0 (on a scale of 5.0). The funds, typically $25,000 or more, are used to purchase books for the library in honor of the achievement of those students. The Chancellor's Parents Fund supported the development of Electric Undergrad, an interactive computer introduction to the library.

5. Interactive Media Site

The interactive media site, established in 1991, provides students and faculty access to interactive media software and resources. Interactive media technology combines the retrieval power of a microcomputer with the visual and audio information accessible through videodisks. One major resource available at the site is the *Video Encyclopedia of the 20th Century,* a powerful research and teaching tool. As more faculty develop their own interactive software programs, the library will move to support a multimedia reserve collection similar to the reserve services currently provided for books, periodicals, software, and traditional audiovisual materials. The Interactive Media Site was stimulated by pioneering work done by chemistry faculty in instructional applications of interactive media and funded through emerging technology grants, a Friends gift, and donations from parent organizations.

6. Media Services

The media center, established in 1977, contains much of the non-print material acquired by the library system. Collaboratively developed with the instructional media campus office for self-directed, individualized instruction, its resources in cinema studies, literature, theater, history, chemistry, and other subject areas are heavily used by students. The viewing area contains videocassette and videodisk playback equipment and television monitors that provide access to the large collection of films, plays, and nonfiction video recordings. Slide–sound and filmstrip–sound projectors, as well as audiocassette players, are available for use within the Undergraduate Library. Media expertise throughout campus is brought to bear in the planning and delivery of media services.

7. Microcomputer Laboratory

Since 1987, the microcomputer lab has provided students with open access to IBM and Macintosh microcomputers. The lab is available, on a first-come, first-served basis, whenever the Undergraduate Library is open. Assistance with the hardware, software, and network access is provided by student technologists. The microcomputer lab is a cooperative venture of the library and Computer Services Office with CSO providing substantial networking technical expertise. Support has also been provided by awards offered on a competitive basis through the campus computer fund.

8. Self-Help Information Center

The self-help information center (SHIC), established in 1983, addresses the personal information needs of undergraduates. It provides students with current pamphlets, books, and media materials on topics related to health, personal growth, self-awareness, and academic skills. The Center also contains a number of computer-based programs: Dilemma Counseling System, a generic problem-solving expert system designed to help students solve problems in logical and systematic ways; SigiPlus, a career guidance and information system; and Health Hazards Appraisal. Student counselors trained in interviewing techniques and campus resources comprise the staff of SHIC. They provide an open, non-threatening environment for counseling and for consultation of SHIC materials, and are trained to refer students in need of more intensive assistance to the appropriate professional counseling services available elsewhere on campus. SHIC is a cooperative effort supported by the library and the campus counseling center.

9. Writers' Workshop

The writers' workshop, established in 1989, provides an opportunity for students, faculty, and staff of all disciplines and levels to discuss writing with tutors who are both experienced writers and teachers of writing. Services are available either by appointment or on a walk-in basis. The workshop is a cooperative initiative of the Undergraduate Library, the Department of English, the Center for the Study of Writing, and the Office of the Vice-Chancellor for Academic Affairs.

Collection Development in Transition

Stephen E. Atkins and Patricia F. Stenstrom

Even in the United States there will presumably come a
time when growth [of collections] must have a stop.[1]

The American academic library, as we think of it today, came into
being at the end of the nineteenth century. Before this time, these
libraries consisted of small, narrowly focused gift collections managed
part-time by faculty members. A new emphasis on research in academe
created a demand for larger institutionally supported collections cover-
ing a broad range of subjects.[2] Faculty members continued to select
materials for their disciplines until sometime after mid-century. However, as disciplines became more specialized and fragmented, librarians
became the selectors. Today, the proper selection of library materials is
one of the most important and demanding tasks of academic librarians. It is a task that requires a thorough knowledge of the information
needs of library users.

Academic Library Users

The primary users of academic libraries are students, undergraduate
and graduate, and faculty. Other groups—alumni, visiting students and
scholars, and local citizens—sometimes use them, but the library's collections are selected to meet the research and instructional needs of
faculty and students.

Undergraduate students are the most numerous users of the library collection. They come to the library to work on classroom assignments. The faculty and librarians see independent learning as an objective of the library, but students do not use the library in this manner. Studies indicate that "students left on their own to use the library for academic purposes, did not make even minimum use of this resource even though the faculty very strongly expected such usage."[3] In a 1991 telephone survey of undergraduates at the University of Illinois at Urbana-Champaign, 81 percent chose "Go to look for information for a class assignment such as a term paper"[4] as a reason for going to the University Library. In this survey, seniors were the most frequent users of the library. Freshmen and juniors were almost tied for second, and sophomores were last.[5] Findings from other surveys are similar to the Illinois survey.

Freshmen often use the library for the first time when they write term papers for composition or rhetoric courses. Many students choose topics in the news, ones of current social interest.[6] These freshmen descend on the library in droves, needing instruction in research techniques, as well as orientation to the library. Reference and other public service librarians are more familiar with these needy freshmen than with other undergraduate users. Other undergraduate library use is also course driven, but usually related to the subject of the course. Their library use is similar to use by graduate students and faculty in the same discipline.[7] Undergraduates need diverse materials including monographs, serials, and electronic databases, and they also need a place for social exchange and study. Accessible collections with an ample supply of current materials suit their needs. Browsing is especially important to undergraduates; they have to develop their research topics and are not proficient in the use of bibliographic tools.[8] CD-ROM and online databases create new demand from undergraduates for more and different resources, particularly more serial titles.

Graduate students use the library to complete research papers for advanced courses or theses. Research on library use by graduate students is limited to citation analysis of graduate students' theses[9] and surveys of library satisfaction.[10] These studies confirm what librarians already know from experience. Graduate students are heavy users of library resources, and the way they use the library is determined by discipline. Master's students' use of the library is similar to use by upper-class undergraduates. Doctoral students spend their graduate careers in the library, the laboratory, or both. They use the library not only to pursue their own research but also as research assistants for faculty members. Because they have had neither time nor money to build personal libraries, they rely more on the library than the faculty. Graduate students want a responsive system that allows them to identify and obtain materials with as little fuss as possible. They become dissatisfied with systems that frustrate speedy access. Despite turnover, as seasoned students graduate and a new crop begins, the demand for timely acquisition of unique materials continues. Graduate students' library experiences last a lifetime. Former graduate students, now new faculty members, expect their new library to match the resources and services of their former library. New faculty members faced with an inferior collection may become dissatisfied users.

The last primary constituency of the library, the faculty, uses the collections for research in their area of expertise and to support assigned teaching responsibilities. Research on scholarly communication has revealed more about faculty use of the library than is known about student use. *Scholarly communication* is the term used to describe the formal and informal ways that ideas and knowledge are transferred within the scholarly community. The earliest studies of scholarly communication concentrated on the information-seeking and dissemination patterns of scientists and engineers; subsequent studies investigated social scientists; and recently, humanists have been the subject of research.[11] Studies of scholarly communication explain the different models for research and learning that exist among broad subject areas and describe the way scholars use libraries. The faculty is divided in its approach to the library. Humanities' faculties regard the library as integral to their success as scholars and teachers, and believe that large library collections with diverse holdings are necessary for research. They consider the library a "center for learning, not just a support for the educational activity that takes place in the classroom."[12] Citation studies indicate that humanities' researchers rely on books more than on journal articles for their research needs.[13] Other studies suggest that these scholars identify what they use first from references in publications, second from communications from colleagues, third from formal bibliography; and fourth from librarians.[14]

Social science fields are not homogeneous. These fields have different approaches to scholarship and research. As a result, they vary in their use of the library. Political scientists, as an example, use the library more than psychologists do.[15] Social scientists do not use the library to locate information but, rather, as a source of supply for information already identified.[16] They use more periodicals than the humanists, but they also use monographs and rely heavily on bibliographies and footnotes in journals and books for locating references.[17] Although all disciplines change their methodologies and focus from time to time, social scientists are especially prone to theoretical change. Disciplines such as political science and sociology that heavily emphasized quantitative methods in the 1960s and 1970s, have now turned to less positivistic approaches.[18] These changes may influence the way that scholars in the social sciences use the library.

A significant portion of the science and engineering faculties finds the library less important than their laboratories. One scholar explained it this way: "Whereas many humanist scholars spend much of their working lives in the library building, for most scientists, engineers and professionals a visit to the library is a special event."[19] Many scientists are uncomfortable in libraries and have devised ways to avoid using them. They place books on reserve as background reading, but monographic literature is usually out of date by the time it is published. Scientists find current information by browsing in journals.[20] They rely on unpublished research papers and conference proceedings for reports of the latest research and depend on preprints for this information. Some preprints are now distributed electronically on the Internet.[21] However, librarians who often have humanities backgrounds expect scientists to be more responsive to the electronic distribution of information than they are. Although the need for current information makes some scientists and engineers receptive to electronic databases in their fields of specialty, "word of mouth and their own library of information" is given preference by most "when they seek information."[22]

Current Trends

The twenty or so years that followed the Second World War were a period of expansion and affluence in both academe and academic libraries. There was ample money to meet users needs and to select on the basis of "possible need." Gradually, imperceptibly at first, this changed. Although campuses increased library funding, the increases did not match inflation. A recent study of the Association of Research Libraries shows that between 1981 and 1995 the buying power of these libraries had declined by 38 percent.[23] In addition, the ever-increasing costs of automation eroded materials budgets. Although sympathetic with the plight of libraries, campuses that faced declining real-dollar support and increasing costs of technological development did not increase allocations.

Although the buying power of libraries has declined, the number of monographs and serials (domestic and international) published annually has increased. A recent edition of *Ullrich's International Periodical Directory* contains information about 165,000 serial titles, but even this exhaustive list may underestimate the total by as much as 15 percent.[24] Publishing is currently dominated by a small number of companies, many with corporate offices outside the United States. As a result, the prices of monographs and serials published abroad are at the mercy of a fluctuating dollar. Serials have had a higher rate of inflation than any other segment of the U.S. economy, including medical care, college tuition, prescription drugs, and auto insurance. Studies of the costs of scientific journals indicate that the pricing policies of foreign commercial publishers are responsible for the escalation in journal prices.[25] These publishers have based prices for serials on perceived value rather than on cost.[26] Publishing entrepreneur Robert Maxwell created the paradigm, now named for him, that "libraries would pay almost any price for premier publications."[27] The paradigm is based on the assumption that despite increases in the price of a journal subscription, either the demand for it remains constant or, if some libraries cancel, publishers can compensate by raising the price for the libraries that continue to subscribe. Librarians cannot easily combat huge serial increases because many costly serials are an integral part of the scholarly communication system. The scholarly communication system operates independently of libraries and yet depends on them to purchase and archive publications. Peer review, "whereby authorities in a given field determine the validity and assess the relative significance of a particular contribution of a scholar or scientist within that field,"[28] is central to the scholarly communication system. The scholarly communication marketplace "is characterized by producers (academic scholars) who turn over gratis, through copyright transfer, the ownership of their products (scholarly journal articles) to sellers (scholarly publishers), who in turn earn a profit, not by selling to the ultimate consumers (again academic scholars), but to publicly supported agencies (academic libraries) acting on behalf of the entire scholarly community to organize, store, and provide free or low-cost access to these products."[29]

In addition to the loss of purchasing power for traditional library materials, costs of electronic information are increasing. Many bibliographic databases are also available on CD-ROM, are locally mounted, or are accessible through the World Wide Web. These databases have superior searching capabilities and are usually available in more locations than their site-dependent paper counterparts. Users' requests for library materials and services have increased because of the widespread availability of these tools. Users demand has intensified competition for budgetary resources among collections, "access services," and equipment.[30]

Competing Needs

The primary users of the library have different needs and motivations in their use of the library. During affluent years following the Second World War, librarians built research collections of books, journals, newspapers, and nonprint formats to anticipate possible demand. "Possible need" or "just-in case" was the guiding principle of collection development, and collection size was used as a measure of quality. In 1944, Fremont Rider predicted that research collection would double every sixteen years.[31] Today, financial and technological forces have slowed the growth of libraries from the rate that Fremont Rider predicted,[32] and collection development librarians are attempting to reconcile a history of exponential growth based on lavish spending with a gradually increasing austerity.

Collection development librarians acknowledge the economic and technological changes that have occurred, but they have yet to formulate a collection development philosophy to replace the comfortable just-in-case philosophy. The academic library world is in the midst of a debate about whom the library should serve and why that pits the competing needs of one user group against another. Are faculty served at the expense of students? Should users who come to the library receive preferential treatment over those who prefer or need remote access? Is it appropriate to cut monograph budgets important to humanists to finance the very expensive science serials?

Some of the debate centers on the role of electronic information. Technological enthusiasts believe that the totally digital library is either here or just around the corner. Their Luddite opponents argue that the electronic revolution is more glitter than substance and that archiving print on paper remains the primary function of the library. Librarians accept technology as a tool to expedite library operations. But technology is increasingly something more than a tool, and some librarians are not comfortable with technology when it is a revolutionary force changing the way people obtain and use information. McLuhan described electronic media as "non-lineal, repetitive, discontinuous, intuitive, proceeding by analogy instead of sequential argument."[33] Many librarians and many users prefer the linear world of the codex to the "paperless society"; they deny that a revolution is in progress and argue that advocates of technology discount its limitations and overestimate the speed of change.

Academic administrators also debate collection development, less because they use the library and more because libraries have an insatiable need for additional allocations. Library users are rarely aware of the library's financial problems because they do not control or provide resources for the library and have a dim and self-centered perception of the issues. They are, however, concerned about the decline of library resources and look for a scapegoat. Technology is often singled out as that scapegoat.

In recent years, library literature has included many articles offering solutions to the crisis in collection development. Some commonly proposed solutions are: resource-sharing and document delivery; new sources of revenue; a revamped scholarly communication system; and reliance on electronic publishing. These national and global solutions have, to date, met with half-hearted acceptance and unacknowledged success because many librarians and users continue to deny the need for change.

As a result of the decline in buying power for libraries, interlibrary lending and borrowing has been increasing at a rapid rate.[34] Depending on definition, resource-sharing is either succeeding or struggling. If resource-sharing means formal structures to expedite interlibrary loan, then enormous progress in resource-sharing has occurred in the past twenty-five years. National bibliographic utilities, OCLC and RLIN, as well as numerous regional and local consortia, have revolutionized the ease of access and speed of borrowing. Some states, Illinois and Ohio are examples, have furthered resource-sharing through financial support. If resource-sharing means cooperative collection development, then it is a problem and has been so for nearly fifty years.[35] Cooperative collection development attempts to rationalize resource-sharing through interlibrary agreements that may: (1) divide collection responsibilities among member libraries, (2) share the costs of expensive purchases or, (3) support centers for the provision of resources.[36] Concerns over local autonomy have limited the success of cooperative collection development. The most successful examples of such cooperation involve libraries in close enough geographic proximity to allow their users ease of access. Efforts to create a national plan have failed because of distance, concern over local autonomy, and questions about financing.

Many librarians believe that because document delivery is less expensive than ownership, it can be a substitute for subscriptions to journals that are either little used, expensive, or both. When a newly developed process, xerography, made it possible to photocopy documents in the 1960s, libraries that had previously been unwilling to loan journals and other restricted items were willing to make copies of articles to send to requesting libraries. Document delivery became one of the services offered by the interlibrary loan department. Although it is closely related to interlibrary loan, document delivery is different from traditional ILL in several respects. First, users who request documents are allowed to keep them; second, the library that provides the copy often charges a fee to recover costs of copying even though it does not charge fees for interlibrary loan; and finally, document delivery is governed by copyright law. Document delivery has become increasingly efficient through the years. Despite this, many faculty members are unwilling, as yet, to accept it as a substitute for ownership. In addition, copyright provisions that restrict the number of copies that can be borrowed from the same journal also limit its use.

At one time, universities maintained partial control of the scholarly communication system by sponsoring scholarly serial publications. However, in the late 1960s and 1970s, universities stopped sponsoring many of these publications. Ironically, librarians and others in the university are urging academe to reclaim control of the process. In 1992, the prestigious Mellon Report discussed options that called for universities to play a more proactive role in the scholarly communication system by retaining control of copyright. [37] The report also envisioned ways that electronic publishing could separate the issue of access from ownership.[38] However, electronic publishing is still in the developmental stage, and problems of peer review, cost recovery, copyright, and credit for promotion have yet to be worked out. Copyright is a particularly thorny issue with publishers arguing for the right to control electronic transmission, downloading, and offprinting, whereas groups such as the ALA argue for less control.

Charging fees and soliciting gifts and contributions are two ways that libraries have sought to add to their revenues. Fees have been most commonly charged for online services, photocopying, and interlibrary lending. Online searching is decreasing because users can do their own searching on free CD-ROM and databases locally mounted or accessed through the Web. Fees for interlibrary transactions are affected by reciprocal lending agreements that reduce income from lending and the costs to the library of borrowing them from other institutions, and often are not passed on to the users. Fees for photocopying are widely accepted, and some institutions make a profit from them. Recently, libraries have tried other types of fees, such as offering extra service to a targeted clientele. Local businesses or professions are singled out for this provision of fees for service. Some institutions charge student user fees, but these may be part of basic funding rather than additional revenue. On the other hand, some libraries have long used gifts and contributions to strengthen their holdings, and more and more libraries are formalizing their fund-raising activities.

Collection development librarians, instinctively archival, worry that in meeting present needs they may not anticipate future needs or sustain previously strong collections that are no longer heavily used. They also worry about preserving texts that are only published electronically. These are reasonable concerns, but ones that must be addressed through national or regional planning. Cooperation among libraries is an essential aspect of this planning, and academic libraries need to give it their wholehearted support. Cooperative collection development fails when it superimposes an overall plan that ignores local user needs and does not also make easy access a high priority. In other words, cooperative collection development should not attempt to satisfy current local demand but, rather, should provide easy, quick access to little used materials such as old textbooks, ephemera, or works in less-used languages through document delivery, interlibrary loan, and electronic archives. Research libraries that support these little-used collections need to take a leadership role in developing cooperative plans and reasonable financial arrangements.

Preservation of electronic texts is a potential problem. Many libraries, for example, cling to paper copies of indexes that are never used because they fear that something will happen to the electronic version, that alternative print sources will disappear, and that technology will change causing some sources to become unusable because appropriate hardware and software will be unavailable. Although these concerns have some validity, some risks are inevitable. Just as libraries struggle to preserve collections printed on acidic papers, in the future, they will struggle to deal with old technologies. In the meantime, libraries cannot ignore current user needs in order to avoid unknown future contingency.

User-Centered Collection Development

College and university libraries carry out collection development activities in a variety of ways. In some, responsibilities are centralized in a single department, but in others, they are decentralized. Branch librarians, subject specialists, or members of the reference department may be collection development librarians. In small college libraries, the library director may do all the selection. Until recently, most larger universities had directors or assistant university librarians for collection development, but cost-cutting has eliminated some of these positions and may eliminate more in the future. In the past, faculty often had significant control over collection development and, of course, many still do recommend purchases, but the era when faculty dominated selection has passed. A study of faculty and librarian selectors in the mid-1980s found that materials selected by librarians circulated more frequently than materials selected by faculty.[39] At the same time, collection development librarians seldom have enough specialized knowledge to collect in depth in all areas of scholarship. This can contribute to homogeneity among collections.

The success of a library in meeting user demand for collections rarely depends on organizational structure. The knowledge and skill of the selector rather than organizational structure are key to the development of high-quality user-oriented collections. In the affluent decades that followed the Second World War, blanket order plans and comprehensive selection replaced the thoughtful review of materials. Today, librarians use a more hands-on approach to selection.

It is far easier to consult the faculty and graduate students than it is to consult undergraduates. The faculty often tell librarians what they need. In addition, in many colleges and universities, teaching departments appoint faculty members to serve as liaisons with the library. The liaisons may be a committee or an individual. The liaison meets with the responsible collection development librarian to pass on book, journal, or database requests from members of the department and to discuss department concerns related to collection development. Meetings with faculty enable selectors to learn more about current faculty research. However, if selectors only talk to faculty who come to them, they will have an incomplete understanding of faculty needs.

Selectors can also go to the faculty, using both formal and informal strategies. To learn more about research or curricular needs, meetings with department heads or selected faculty can be useful. Reading faculty research; maintaining files of faculty awards and grants; and attending department or university lectures and symposia are additional ways to become informed. A variety of research techniques are also available to measure use of materials by faculty and students. Automated circulation systems can measure collection use by classification numbers;[40] other techniques measure in-house-use;[41] and interlibrary borrowing requests can be scrutinized to identify collection weaknesses. Citations in faculty publications can be compared to library holdings. This technique evaluates the collection in an area of faculty research.

Graduate students sometimes funnel their requests though an advisor because they feel that faculty requests receive more serious attention. At other times, the requests arrive directly from the student. Resourceful graduate students, especially those completing a doctorate, make appointments with the collection development librarian to discuss their research proposals. Graduate students often conduct research on topics related to their faculty advisor's research, and the collection development librarian may already be collecting in associated areas. Collection development librarians can reach out to graduate students at university-, department-, or library-sponsored orientation programs. This is an opportunity to explain selection policies and the way to request materials.

Few requests come from undergraduates. Undergraduate students can rarely plan their research far enough in advance to request and obtain materials in time to meet their deadlines. Often the students lack the research and bibliographic skills to locate materials not readily available and therefore conduct their research with those on hand. Collection development librarians can anticipate need. Because undergraduate use is curriculum driven, collection development librarians can utilize their knowledge of faculty research and teaching, review circulation records and reserve reading lists, and talk to reference librarians about current assignments and popular research. Volunteering to work at a reference desk is a good way to become informed.

Librarians sympathetic to the difficulties freshmen encounter in their first research projects often conclude that undergraduates are shortchanged at the expense of the faculty and argue for "basic, general materials on popular topics."[42] But the freshmen term paper, though probably the student's first and most unnerving use of the collection, should not be the last, and general material on popular topics will not serve upper-class users. Part of the rationale for acquiring material to meet freshmen needs is that scholarly material is obtuse or esoteric. This is true of some scholarly writing, but not all. Well-written material based on research may challenge freshmen, but that is precisely what it should do. The collection development librarian cannot ignore the needs of undergraduates, especially freshmen. They do, however, need to pay special attention to quality in their selection.

In selecting monographs for undergraduates, carefully monitored approval plans can be quite helpful. Approval plans have gained wide acceptance because they offer discounts and faster receipt of new titles. Use of these plans, however, does not release selectors from the responsibility of knowing current literature and evaluating it. Approval plans need ongoing evaluation. Selectors should review new approval plan books as they are received and compare approval plan selections against reliable book reviews. Selection does, after all, demand evaluation and decision making based on knowledge and judgment.

To meet student and other user needs, it is often necessary to buy multiple copies of good works in high demand rather than exclusively acquiring single copies. Selectors can also concentrate on works not readily available in inexpensive paperback editions rather than those works that are. Works published by advocacy groups can enrich the collections. Many advocacy groups publish monographs and tracts that argue for their point of view and are very reasonably priced. Obviously, the selector will want to obtain publications that represent more than one point of view, but these publications can add needed strength to collections in certain areas.

Serial use by undergraduates is increasing because electronic periodical indexes, such as those available on CD-ROM, are so much more user-friendly. The increased use has created demand for new serials and increased use of older serials. Sometimes students identify serials not available in the library based on citations from these indexes. It is important that both collection development and reference librarians make an effort to know the quality and depth of information in serials indexed on electronic databases. Collection development librarians can request sample issues. Circulating these sample issues to the reference staff will give them alternatives to compare to the current collection. They can then endorse new titles and recommend the cancellation of current titles. The reference staff will also be better able to advise students working with long indiscriminate bibliographies garnered from electronic versions of indexes of the merit of various sources. Students will accept, even welcome, microform or full-text electronic articles in place of paper ones if the microform or full-text editions are accessible and have print capabilities. Paper collections of heavily used journals are often dog-eared, vandalized, and incomplete. Microform and electronic copies do not suffer such damage. In comparing full-text or microform collections to paper collections, the cost of processing, preserving, and storing paper should be considered. Students, who pay to photocopy paper sources, will expect to pay to print or download from full-text and microform sources.

Colleges and universities are not democratic. The faculty control the curriculum and in doing so should have a powerful influence on the content of the collection. Larry Hardesty and Collette Mak found that this affected core collections held by college libraries. These core collections were extremely small, and there was little overlap among noncore materials. Hardesty and Mak explain that "lack of overlap is a reflection of the idiosyncratic nature of the undergraduate curriculum that, in turn, is a reflection of the idiosyncratic nature of the college faculty."[43] The size of the faculty and complexity of curriculum in universities together with acquisitions' strategies such as blanket order plans make research library collections somewhat more homogeneous, but within even these collections, true strength is the result of a strong curriculum or faculty influence. Because the faculty determine what students study and research, students' library use will for the most part mirror faculty research and teaching interests. The authors make this point to set aside the argument that faculty and student collection needs are inherently conflicting. Their need for reference service, bibliographic control, and access may be in conflict, but their collection needs should be quite similar.

Requests to order materials from users deserve serious attention. Purchase is the obvious choice for monographic works that require long-term use, but interlibrary loan may be the choice if the user is uncertain about the usefulness of a particular document or only needs to consult it briefly. Interlibrary borrowing is an integral component of collection development. Sound collection development requires a review of interlibrary borrowing patterns. Perhaps libraries should re-evaluate organizational structure combining collection development, interlibrary borrowing, and document delivery into a single administrative structure.

Some faculty are more aggressive than others in requesting monographic purchases, but selectors need not become concerned about equity as long as the faculty-at-large are fully aware of their right to make requests. Selectors may question the appropriateness of some suggestions. Unfortunately, reviews will not usually answer their concerns. Yvla Lindholm-Romantschuk found that scholarly monographs do not generate many reviews; that the number of reviews is affected by the prestige of the publisher; that the rate of review varies by discipline; and that a small core of journals in each field determines the direction of that field.[44] She also confirmed what every collection development librarian knows, that most reviews appear one to two years after publication.[45] When there are questions about the appropriateness of a purchase, conversation with the requesting faculty may be the best way to get the information needed to make a decision.

The cost of new serials may prevent their acquisition, unless currently held titles are canceled. Selectors are faced with a difficult decision when they receive a request to purchase a serial title. They can request sample issues and can consult the departmental liaison for an opinion on the usefulness of the title to a discipline. If the title is interdisciplinary, several interested groups can be consulted. If the title does not fit into the collection, if it lacks a sufficient audience, if it is not of high enough quality, the collection development librarian may deny the request. However, serial collections need continuous reevaluation. It is difficult to cancel a journal that has been in the collection from volume one, but serials change in scope and quality. In some cases, the subject matter is now irrelevant or a new serial covers the topic better. Faculties, as well as librarians, are sometimes guilty of sentimentality about library holdings. Some works or types of works are revered not because they are used, but because of mystique. Tina E. Chrzastowski, Paul M. Blobaum, and Margaret A. Welshmer have illustrated this phenomenon in their discussion of 'Beilstein.'[46] The same authors stress the importance of communicating with the user, offering hard data about the use of materials and the consequences to the collection of retaining little-used, expensive material.

Document delivery or full-text systems can substitute for subscriptions if the library is unable, because of cost, to subscribe. Because of the inflationary cost of sci-tech journals, they may be ideal candidates for document delivery. Document delivery is, after all, comparable to the system of offprints scientists have used for years. However, many scientists and engineers still prefer to have the paper journals on hand and will need to be persuaded that document delivery is a viable substitute and that continuing some subscriptions entails unreasonable sacrifice.

Serial prices are not an issue with the humanities faculty. Humanities faculties want traditional services. A survey of Modern Language Association members and other associations participating in the American Council of Learned Societies found that what "scholars want librarians to do is maintain primary records in such a way that future scholars who wish to study these artifacts will be able to do so."[47] It is easier to fulfill their requests because they rely on monographs and their journals are less expensive. At the same time, humanists are perhaps the most obsessive proponents of the just-in-case philosophy and need to develop more realistic expectations not only of what the library can buy, but also of what it can afford to put on its shelves.

Social science journals have a higher average cost than humanities' journals, and most disciplines are experiencing a higher rate of inflation than in the humanities. The more dependent on journal literature a discipline is, the higher the cost and the more difficult it is for the library to keep up with demand. For example, the rate of inflation in psychology, a journal-reliant discipline, is comparable to the inflation rate in the sciences. Social sciences books and journals are still less expensive than those in the sciences, and document delivery as substitute for ownership would not be, generally speaking, cost-effective at the present time—but the time may come.

Given the grim, but accurate, picture the authors have painted of current collection development problems, many libraries will be forced to adopt new collection development strategies. National planning and cooperation may alleviate some problems, but only if librarians and users can agree on the future. Unfortunately, future planning not only requires a crystal ball, but belief by viewers that the image in the ball is true. How can libraries proceed? First, librarians need to agree among themselves on a plan for collection development. Treating all users same does not ensure good service or equability. Rather, it is as likely to create bland mediocrity. Collection development librarians often come from the humanities and may be more sympathetic to the humanist; science and technology librarians may favor their users; and reference librarians may favor students, especially undergraduates. Libraries must recognize that these biases are obstacles to service and develop new budgeting models that look at collection development and other access services as a whole to ensure the highest possible level of service for every user. Humanities bibliographers and science bibliographers cannot compete with each other for funds and expect their users to take budget problems seriously.

Next the library needs to enter into a dialog with faculty, students, and campus administrators. Academic libraries depend on the active support of each of these groups, and any library that ignores them will fail. Campus administrations respond to the insensitive treatment of users by interfering in library operations. Librarians can assume a leadership role in explaining the problems the library faces as a result of declining resources. They can also inform their users of the difficult choices and clarify misinformation. Librarians will need to experiment with different strategies, listen attentively to feedback evaluating the experiments, and be prepared to introduce new services incrementally. In the end, they need to arrive at a viable plan that will maximize benefits to the users they serve and be accepted by a majority of those users.

Notes

1. Gordon Ray, "A Retrospective View," in *American Libraries as Centers of Scholarship* (Hanover, N.H.: Dartmouth College, 1978), 28.

2. Stephen Atkins, *The Academic Library in the American University.* (Chicago: ALA, 1991), 3–17.

3. Mary K. Sellen and Jan Jirouch, "Perceptions of Library Use by Faculty and Students: A Comparison," *College & Research Libraries* 45 (July 1984): 264–65.

4. Unpublished survey conducted in Oct. and Nov. 1991 of a stratified probability sample of 221 undergraduate students selected by the Office of Admissions and Records. Professor D. Charles Whitney was responsible for

the preparation of the survey and the training of the interviewers, and was author of the final report.

5. Unpublished survey completed for the University Library under the direction of Professor D. Charles Whitney.

6. Kathleen Joswick, "Library Use by College Freshmen: A Citation Analysis of Composition Papers," *College and Undergraduate Libraries* 1 (1994): 54.

7. Rose Mary Magrill and Gloriana St. Clair, "Undergraduate Term Paper Citation Patterns by Disciplines and Level of Course," *Collection Management* 12, nos. 3–4 (1990): 25–56.

8. Barbara Valentine, "Undergraduate Research Behavior: Using Focus Groups to Generate Theory," *Journal of Academic Librarianship* 19, no. 5 (Nov. 1993): 302-3.

9. See, for example, Joy Thomas, "Graduate Student Use of Journals: A Bibliometric Study of Psychology Theses," *Behavioral and Social Sciences Librarian* 12, no. 1 (winter 1993): 1–7.

10. For example, "A Day in the Life of the USC Libraries," in *SPEC Kit, 205: User Surveys in Libraries*, comp. Elaine Brekke (Washington, D.C.: Association of Research Libraries, Office of Management Studies, 1994), 183–85.

11. Abdelmajid Bouazza, "Information User Studies," in *Encyclopedia of Library and Information Science*, Vol. 44 (New York: Marcel Dekker, 1989), 144.

12. Ray L. Heffner, "Zero Growth: When Is Not-Enough Enough? A Symposium," *Journal of Academic Librarianship* 1 (Nov. 1975): 5.

13. *Scholarly Communication: The Report of the National Enquiry* (Baltimore: Johns Hopkins Pr., 1979), 45.

14. Stephen E. Wiberley Jr. and William G. Jones, "Patterns of Information Seeking in the Humanities," *College & Research Libraries* 50 (Nov. 1989): 638–45.

15. Bouazza, "Information User Studies," 151.

16. Ibid.

17. Patricia F. Stenstrom and Ruth B. McBride, "Serial Use by Social Science Faculty: A Survey," *College & Research Libraries* 40 (Sept. 1979): 429.

18. Constance C. Gould and Mark Handler, *Information Needs in the Social Sciences: An Assessment* (Mountain View, Calif.: Research Libraries Group, 1989).

19. William Y. Arms, "Scholarly Publishing on the National Networks," *Scholarly Publishing* 23 (Apr. 1992): 159.

20. J. F. B. Rowland, "The Scientist's View of His Information System," *Journal of Documentation* 38 (Mar. 1982): 1–40.

21. D. Dallman, M. Draper, and S. Schwarz, "Electronic Pre-publishing for Worldwide Access: The Case of High Energy Physics," *Interlending and Document Supply* 22, no. 2 (1994): 3–7.

22. Maurita Peterson Holland and Christina Kelleher Powell, "A Longitudinal Survey of the Information Seeking and User Habits of Some Engineers," *College & Research Libraries* 56 (Jan. 1995): 13.

23. Brian L. Hawkins, "The Unsustainability of the Traditional Library and the Threat to Higher Education,", (paper presented at the Stanford Forum on Higher Education Futures, Aspen Institute, Aspen Meadows, Colo., Oct. 18, 1996).

24. This underreporting of serial titles was noted as far back as the late 1970's. William H. Webb, "Collection Development for the University and Large Research Library: More and More versus Less and Less," in *Academic Libraries by the Year 2000: Essays Honoring Jerrold Orne*, ed. Herbert Poole (New York & London: Bowker, 1977), 140–41.

25. Kenneth E. Marks, Steven P. Nielsen, and H. Craig Petersen, "Longitudinal Study of Scientific Journal Prices in a Research Library," *College & Research Libraries* 52 (Mar. 1991): 137.

26. Paul Metz and Paul M. Gherman, "Serial Pricing and the Role of the Electronic Journal," *College & Research Libraries* 52 (July 1991): 318.

27. Joseph J. Esposito, "The Future of Publishing," *ARL* 178 (Jan. 1995):2.

28. Charles B. Osborn, "The Structuring of the Scholarly Communication System," *College & Research Libraries* 50 (May 1989). 279.

29. Gary D. Byrd, "An Economic 'Commons' Tragedy for Research Libraries: Scholarly Journal Publishing and Pricing Trends," *College & Research Libraries* 51 (May 1990): 189.

30. Dilys E. Morris, "Electronic Information and Technology: Impact and Potential for Academic Libraries," *College & Research Libraries* 50 (Jan. 1989): 61.

31. Fremont Rider, *The Scholar and the Future of the Research Library* (New York: Hadham, 1944), 3.

32. Richard Hume Werking, "Collection Growth and Expenditures in Academic Libraries: A Preliminary Inquiry," *College & Research Libraries* 52 (1991): 9–11.

33. Lewis H. Lapham, "Introduction," in Marshall McLuhan, *Understanding Media* (Cambridge, Mass.: MIT, 1994), iv.

34. Barbara B. Higginbotham and Sally Bowdoin, *Access versus Assets* (Chicago: ALA, 1993), 10–12.

35. George Alan Works, *College and University Library Problems* (Chicago: ALA, 1927), ix–x.

36. Joseph J. Branin, "Cooperative Collection Development," in *Collection Management: A New Treatise*, ed. Charles B. Osburn and Ross Atkinson (Greenwich, Conn.: JAI Pr., 1991), 104–7.

37. Anthony M. Cummings, Marcia L. Witte, William G. Bowen, Laura O. Lazarus, and Richard H. Ekman, *University Libraries and Scholarly Communication: A Study Prepared for the Andrew W. Mellon Foundation* (Washington, D.C.: Association of Research Libraries, 1992), xxviii.

38. Ibid., xxiii; Ross Atkinson, "Text Mutability and Collection Administration," *Library Acquisitions: Theory and Practice* 14 (1990): 355–58.

39. Tschera Harkness Connell, "Comparing the Circulation of Library Materials Ordered by Faculty and Librarians," *Collection Management* 14, nos. 1–2 (1991): 83.

40. For a discussion of the use of automated systems in collection analysis, see F.W. Lancaster and Beth Sandore, "Automated Systems in Collection Management," in *Technology Management in Library and Information Services* (Champaign, Ill.: Univ. of Illinois Graduate School of Library and Information Science, 1997), 55–82.

41. F.W. Lancaster, "In-house Use," in *If You Want to Evaluate Your Library*, 2nd. ed. (Champaign, Ill.: Univ. of Illinois Graduate School of Library and Information Science, 1993), 76–86.

42. "Library Use by College Freshmen," 64

43. Larry Hardesty and Collette Mak, "Searching for the Holy Grail: A Core Collection for Undergraduate Libraries," *Journal of Academic Librarianship* 19 (Jan. 1994): 367.

44. Ylva Lindholm-Romantschuk, "The Flow of Ideas within and among Academic Disciplines: Scholarly Book Reviewing in the Social Sciences and Humanities (Ph.D. diss., Univ. of California-Berkeley, 1994), 192–93.

45. Lindholm-Romantschuk "The Flow of Ideas," 170.

46. Tina E. Chrzastowski, Paul M. Blobaum, and Margaret A. Welshmer, "Cost/Use Analysis of Beilstein's *Handbuch der organischen Chemie* at Two Academic Chemistry Libraries," *Serials Librarian* 20, no. 4 (1991): 80–81.

47. Stanford G. Thatcher, "Toward the Year 2001," *Scholarly Publishing* 24 (Oct. 1992): 25–37.

Cataloging: A Case Study of
Self-Imposed Obsolescence

Patricia F. Stenstrom

While cataloging skills were presented as a universal good,
no one discussed how they should be employed beyond
traditional tasks. Rather than feeling uplifted, I walked
away with a sense of foreboding; I had seen the enemy and
it was us.[1]

T he author was a full-time cataloger for a number of years and
cataloged part-time for many more. Cataloging was enjoyable and
work as a cataloger made her a far better reference and collection development librarian. Yet, writing about user centered cataloging in aca
demic libraries is a dismal task because cataloging is not user centered
and truly has not been since the Library of Congress began to mass-
produce catalog cards. In the "Preface to the Fourth Edition" of his
Rules for a Dictionary Catalog, Charles A. Cutter wrote:

> The Library of Congress has begun to furnish its printed
> cards on such liberal terms that any new library would be
> foolish not to make its catalog mainly of them, and older
> libraries find them a valuable assistance in the cataloging of
> their accessions, not so much because they are cheaper as
> because in the case of most libraries they are better than the
> library is likely to make itself.[2]

By 1909, 1,200 libraries were subscribing to LC cards,[3] and that number grew every year until 1968, when there were 25,000 subscribers.[4] Economy was the primary motivation in the widespread use of the LC cards. Accepting the Library of Congress as the nation's cataloger and arbiter of cataloging practice reduced duplication of effort and undoubtedly standardized the nation's cataloging. However, L.C.'s one-size-fits-all card ignored differences in collections and differences among users; user needs were never a primary motivation, as the following quotation from the 1906 ALA Conference illustrates: "Don't allow yourself to be misled by those who counsel against them [Library of Congress cards] because the fullness of imprint, etc. is confusing to the public."[5] Although LC cards greatly reduced user-centered cataloging, as Richard De Gennaro noted, catalogers were still able to meet the needs of local users because "manual systems easily tolerated local options, inconsistencies, and changing rules."[6]

Another blow to user-centered cataloging, this one nearly fatal, occurred in the 1970s when academic libraries began to depend on national bibliographic utilities, principally OCLC and RLIN, for their cataloging. Library of Congress cataloging was the largest single source of cataloging in these databases, but cataloging from other member libraries added enough additional records so that in all but large research libraries, these bibliographic networks supplied cataloging for more than 90 percent of all of the tiles added to library collections. The bibliographic utilities also heralded the online catalog, giving most catalogers their first experience with machine-readable data.

The card catalog replaced the book catalog at the beginning of the twentieth century, part of a movement orchestrated by Melville Dewey, to make libraries more efficient. The virtues of the card catalogs over book catalogs were currency, flexibility, and responsiveness to change. For a time, these virtues compensated for the card catalog's weaknesses, "immobility, complexity, destructibility, and steadily rising costs of maintenance."[7] In the end, by the late 1960s, weakness overcame strength and the card catalog collapsed under the weight of cataloging and filling arrearages.[8] Some libraries experimented with computer generated book and microform catalogs, but by the end of the 1980s, most academic libraries had replaced their card catalogs with an online catalog (often called OPAC, or online public access catalog). How have online catalogs affected users, and how have catalogers responded?

Catalog Use Studies

Several literature reviews provide summaries of the many online catalog user studies that have been conducted in the past two decades.[9] These user studies employed surveys, transaction logs, and observations in a variety of settings, although recently published research relied on focus groups.[10] Some, such as Sharon Seymour, have criticized these studies for poor design and lack of research expertise.[11] Even so, the studies consistently identify the same obstacles to the successful use of online catalogs.

The following brief summary furnishes an overview of important conclusions from user studies, especially those related to academic library users. The highest percentage of catalog use in academic libraries is for class work.[12] Given that undergraduate students constitute the largest proportion of the academic population, this is not surprising. Students prefer online catalogs and use them.[13-14] Student use probably accounts for most subject searches. As might be expected given faculty information-seeking behavior, the faculty uses the catalog most often to find known items, although their use of subject searching may be higher than anticipated.[15]

Early studies indicated that a significant portion of online catalog searches were subject searches.[16] Later studies have confirmed the importance of subject searching,[17] although determining the exact amount is difficult because in studies based on transaction log analysis, it is not always possible to distinguish a true title search from a keyword title search for subjects. Rhonda N. Hunter,[18] Thomas A. Peters,[19] and Patricia M. Wallace[20] have identified problems users experience in searching the catalog. Typographical errors, orthography, and difficulties in using the system were reasons for failure, but the inability to use controlled vocabulary or to think of alternative search terms were also common causes. Numerous studies have shown that users prefer keyword searching to the use of Library of Congress Subject Headings.[21] A finding by Karen Markey that searchers entered "whatever popped in to the searcher mind" when doing subject searches has been corroborated in later studies.[22-23] Failure to consult

Library of Congress Subject Headings is widely reported.[24] Users appear to "interpret the meaning of sub-divided subjects in the same manner as catalogers [interpret them]" only 40 percent of the time.[25]

Users do not find the use of Boolean operators "intuitively obvious."[26] Research also indicates that users find either too much or too little. Stephen E. Wiberley Jr. and Robert Allen Daugherty, in summarizing research about user persistence in scanning OPAC postings, speculate that most users will look at no more than thirty-five postings at a time.[27] Because many OPAC searches produce many more postings than this, the user is frequently frustrated and either gives up or settles for less than the most appropriate sources. Searches that retrieve nothing or too little are equally problematic. In one study of subject keyword searches 34 percent of the searches produced zero hits and 53 percent retrieved only one relevant citation.[28]

A major conclusion to be drawn from numerous research studies is that although users seem to like the online catalog and have a fair degree of success in searching for known items, they experience difficulty in searching by subject.

Cataloger's Response

Catalogers generally do not engage in user studies, and they rarely write about them. Cataloging literature discusses technical aspects of cataloging, management issues, and standards. When user needs are discussed, they are based on the long-held assumptions that users need full records and that these records must be error free. Ruth Hafter explains this very well:

> Central to the cataloging ethos is the fixation on consistency, complexity, quality standards, and quality control based on the interpretation of acknowledged master catalogers. Linked to these factors are the catalogers' strong interest in their peers and their professional standards, and their apparent lack of concern about the library patron.[29]

Catalogers invoke the name of the user in their pursuit of "quality cataloging." "Quality cataloging" is code used to defend current cataloging practice against all arguments for change.[30] As Sarah E. Thomas has noted, the discussion of quality cataloging focuses "on measurable aspects of the bibliographic record—such as accuracy and adherence to rules and rule interpretations, and as she further notes, this emphasis on the measurable minimizes the subjective nature of cataloging."[31]

Is it the search for quality that has made the Library of Congress cataloging an absolute authority? Pat Oddy relates an old joke that catalogers in the United States believe that only two libraries produce good-quality cataloguing—their own and the Library of Congress.[32] In contemporary American cataloging with its heavy reliance on Library of Congress Rule Interpretations, it may be said that only one library, LC, produces quality cataloging.

Library Administrator's Response

Catalogers and administrators have been skirmishing for decades.[33] Administrators want books and other materials cataloged and on the shelves quickly and cheaply. They assumed that computer-based net- worked cataloging would increase production and reduce costs. How- ever, the need of catalogers to validate their expertise by editing non- LC copy and their obsession to add only "perfect" cataloging to na- tional databases did not result in savings or increased efficiency. Faced with passive resistance to change, administrators then created sepa- rate copy cataloging units instructed to maintain high production. In the most recent and drastic move in this ongoing war, some outsourced cataloging; that is, they contracted to have their cata- loging done by commercial firms. Arnold Hirshon succinctly pro- vides the justification for outsourcing. In his view, outsourcing is the solution if it is cheaper and the quality is as good as can be achieved in-house.[34] Although she attempts to be evenhanded, Clare B. Dunkle, in an exceptionally well-documented article, states the case against outsourcing.[35] She argues that cost savings and quality control are questionable. Only in her conclusions does she touch on the heart of the matter: "The catalog may be cheaper, but will it be better? Will it continue to improve, developing and enhancing opportunities for access to information? Will it meet the needs of the next century's users?" She goes on to state: "In-house catalog departments have the opportunity to develop unique solutions for local users, and some of these unique solutions become state of the art."[36]

User-Centered Cataloging

From a user perspective, the purpose of the catalog is to identify and locate books, journals, videos, and other forms of information. The catalog is a means rather than an end. The end is to help people find documents and, ultimately, information or knowledge. At one time, it was a library's most important tool; now it is one of many important tools. The modern online catalog includes order records, holdings, and circulation records, and in many libraries an array of bibliographic databases, as well as the Internet. A few users want, or believe they want, the bibliographic detail of a full catalog record, but most are oblivious to the fine points of a well-crafted record. On the other hand, though critics complain that the International Standard Bibliographic Description (ISBD) is confusing, most academic library users can deal with bibliographic description. Although cataloging theorists debate the importance of the main entry, online information retrieval almost totally obscures its importance to the average user. Access to information is key to user success. Subject headings, classification, and authority control are some important elements in achieving access.

The following steps will make cataloging more user centered: decentralize cataloging operations and increase cataloger's interaction with the public; provide adequate education and training for all librarians and staff; look at the online catalog as a work in progress responsive to change; treat all of the elements of the catalog as an interactive whole; and break the LC habit by being willing to make independent judgments.

Current technology offers academic libraries the opportunity to restructure technical services operations, including cataloging. Because integrated systems readily support decentralization, libraries no longer need to warehouse cataloging operations. Some routine procedures, such as the classification of new editions of current holdings, can be done when the order is placed. A significant portion of copy cataloging can be done in the same way. These routine tasks no longer need to be centralized. A full-time cataloger is not warranted in many smaller academic libraries. Authors of a recent survey report that librarians are increasingly involved in more than one professional activity.[37] Allowing catalogers to use their superior bibliographic skills in reference service and collection development helps users and makes catalogers more aware of users' approach to information-seeking. Further, the shared knowledge and skills of catalogers and other colleagues who have subject, language, or other expertise creates a better catalog.

Reorganization of cataloging is not a new idea. Various approaches have been taken over the years. An effort to decentralize cataloging undertaken at the University of Illinois at Urbana-Champaign in 1982 offers some insight into the problem decentralization many encounter.[38] As part of a reorganization of the then technical services department, catalogers were moved from a centralized cataloging unit into departmental libraries. Original cataloging was to be done in these subject-oriented libraries not only by the transferred catalogers but also by other librarians. In this model, a holistic librarian, a reference librarian no longer stationed at a reference desk, would connect library users with the information or knowledge they needed.[39] In other words, all librarians would become, to use Jerry D. Campbell's somewhat pretentious term, "access engineers."[40]

Holistic librarianship has never completely succeeded. Although catalogers enthusiastically embraced public service activities, public service librarians lacked appropriate training and incentives to learn cataloging rules and MARC tagging. In libraries with trained catalogers, holistic librarianship has been moderately successful. Although some backlogs remain, librarians, knowledgeable about collection use, have cataloging priorities responsive to user needs. In libraries without trained catalogers, holistic librarianship has failed, although even in these units some librarians are interested in assigning call numbers and subject headings. When holistic librarianship functions properly, users benefit from the bibliographic skills of the librarians who have created the catalog and from client-centered subject headings and classification. These benefits outweigh arguments that the cataloging is imperfect.[41] The holistic librarian experience has underscored the importance of education and training, however.

Practitioners often argue that library education places too much emphasis on theory and not enough on practice. However, John J.

Reimer effectively agues that "The perspective that theory provides is essential to the ability to envision, propose, and evaluate possible alternatives to the status quo."[42] Further, because practice is firmly planted in the here and now, practice suited to today may be passé tomorrow. To create user-centered catalogs, librarians must have a broad understanding of bibliographic control. "It is vital that librarians think logically, understand the ways in which knowledge and information are organized for retrieval, and be able to communicate their knowledge of these structures to the library user," according to Michael Gorman.[43] An appropriate education for cataloging might include, in addition to cataloging, courses in information storage and retrieval, indexing and abstracting, bibliography, automation, user education, and information needs assessment—courses that benefit almost all practitioners. The practical aspects of cataloging are better taught in intensive workshops, practicums, and internships. Librarians, who perform work as original catalogers, can choose the training programs that they require to catalog. Although librarians in general may not need as much technical knowledge as cataloging specialists, they do need to understand the way the catalog is structured because creating and maintaining a user centered catalog is everyone's responsibility.

Because revising or otherwise correcting cards in a card catalog was time-consuming and complicated, such changes were discouraged. Although present-day computers make easy revision possible, any changes except for obvious mistakes are still discouraged. If librarians working with the public discover that additional subject headings or cross-references would make a work easier to identify, layers of bureaucratic red tape prevent these additions. Some catalogers proprietarily also resent and resist changes to their cataloging. Subject headings in particular need continuous review. New terms are added and old terms change meaning. The library's public may use different terms for the same thing, depending on the level of specialization or geographic location. Adding terms to the catalog to make it current and to including terminology to fit the vocabularies of different users is common sense. For example, the subject heading Library Orientation is used for "bibliographic instruction" and its acronym BI, even though library orientation and bibliographic instruction mean different things to specialists in the field. In academic libraries, proper use of both these terms would assist the user.

The good old days were not very good bibliographically. Indexes and abstracts in paper cumulated slowly, and a search for journal articles could involve examining a dozen or more volumes. After the articles were identified, another search in the card catalog was required to identify the journals held in the library. If the library did not hold the journal, a new set of tools, such as the *Union List of Serials, New Serial Titles,* or the *National Union Catalog,* were consulted. Given the complexity of the task, only the most motivated users consulted indexes and abstracts. The same was true for other bibliographic sources. The modern online catalog, however, permits one-stop shopping. Some libraries add their journal holdings to bibliographic databases, eliminating the need to move from one database to another, and some databases include not only bibliographic information but full text as well. The public, even the knowledgeable public, cannot distinguish between the online catalog and the other information resources available at the same terminal. Reference and other public service librarians are indexing the Internet for their clientele by setting up home pages and creating links to relevant resources. Catalogers can also use their skills to enhance the retrieval of information. When the bibliographic universe is analyzed, some works in some disciplines receive more comprehensive coverage. If libraries insert local holdings into bibliographic databases, why not link catalog records to bibliographic databases? In works less likely to be indexed, contents are desirable. By treating bibliographic systems as a whole, cataloging can become a powerful tool in making access possible.

There is a popular form of self-help literature that discusses "dependency." All of the ills of dependency are present in the cataloging communities' relationship with the Library of Congress: anxiety about change, unwillingness to take risks, and the inability to think creatively. These characteristics damage catalogers, cataloging, and the general public. Universal bibliographic control (UBC) is a worthy goal and the library world is moving in that direction, but UBC is only reasonably effective for bibliographic description. To believe or even pretend to believe that LC or any institution can singlehandedly provide subject headings and classification for all other institutions is ridiculous.

Most of what is in this chapter has been said before and continues to be said by a variety of observers. Sheila Inter has written about many of these issues in her column in *Technicalities*; Pauline A. Cochrane[44] and Sanford Berman[45] have critically evaluated Library of Congress subject headings; and Michael Buckland has discussed "redefining the catalog."[46] More than ten years ago, Hugh C. Atkinson said of Sanford Berman's efforts to reform subject headings:

> Sanford Berman's long campaign to have libraries provide a language of access that corresponds to the language used by patrons to formulate their requests is essentially correct. Sandy often reminds me of those prophets who wander through the pages of the Old Testament proclaiming the truth so accurately and so irritatingly that the rest of us, while recognizing the validity of the message, wish they would just go away and stop demanding such difficult reforms.[47]

Notes

1. Sherry Vellucci, "Future Catalogers: Essential Colleagues or Anachronisms," *College & Research Library News* 57 (July/Aug. 1996): 442.

2. Charles A Cutter, *Rules for a Dictionary Catalog*, 4th ed. (Washington, D.C.: Government Printing Office, 1904), 5.

3. Herbert Putnam, *Report of the Librarian of Congress for the Fiscal Year Ending June 30, 1909* (Washington, D.C., Government Printing Office, 1909), 53.

4. Charles A. Goodrum, *The Library of Congress*, (New York: Praeger, 1974), 202.

5. *Papers and Proceedings of the 28th General Meeting of the American Library Association, Held at Narragansett Pier, RI. June 29–July 6, 1906* (Boston: ALA, 1906), 266–67.

6. Richard De Gennaro, "Libraries and Networks in Transition: Problems and Prospects for the 1980s," *Library Journal* 106 (May 15, 1981): 1046.

7. Jesse H. Shera, "The Book Catalog and the Scholar—A Reexamination of an Old Partnership," in *Libraries and the Organization of Knowledge* (Hamden, Conn.: Archon Bks., 1965), 152; first published in *Library Resources & Technical Services* 6 (summer 1962): 211.

8. Nicholson Baker, "Discards," *New Yorker* 70 (Apr. 4, 1994): 67.

9. An early review article, Pauline A. Cochrane and Karen Markey, "Catalog Use Studies—Since the Introduction of Online Interactive Catalogs: Impact on Design for Subject Access," *Library and Information Science Research* 5 (winter 1983): 337–63, has been followed by a number of other reviews, most recently by Barbara A. Norgard, Michael G. Berger, Michael K. Buckland, and Christian Plaut, "The Online Catalog: From Technical Service to Access Service," *Advances in Librarianship* 17 (1993): 111–48.

10. Lynn Silipigni Connaway, Debra Wilcox Johnson, and Susan E. Searing, "Online Catalogs from the Users' Perspective: The Use of Focus Group Interviews," *College & Research Libraries* 58 (Sept. 1997): 403–20.

11. Sharon Seymour, "Online Public Access Catalog User Studies: A Review of Research Methodologies, March 1986–November 1989," *Library and Information Science Research* 13 (Apr.–June 1991): 89–102.

12. Karen Markey, *Subject Searching in Library Catalogs: Before and after the Introduction of Online Catalogs.* (Dublin, Ohio: Online Computer Library Center, 1984), 12.

13. See, for example, *Using Online Catalogs: A Nationwide Survey: A Report of a Study Sponsored by the Council on Library Resources*, ed. Joseph R. Mathews, Gary S. Lawrence, and Douglas K. Ferguson (New York: Neal-Schuman, 1983), 153; David Steinberg and Paul Metz, "User Response to and Knowledge about an Online Catalog," *College & Research Libraries* 46 (Jan. 1984): 67.

14. See, for example, Pat Ensor, "User Characteristics of Keyword Searching in an OPAC," *College & Research Libraries* 53 (Jan. 1992): 76; Ingrid Hsieh-Yee, "Student Use of Online Catalogs and Other Information Channels, *College & Research Libraries* 57 (Mar. 1996): 164.

15. Carolyn O. Frost, "Faculty Use of Subject Searching in Card and Online Catalogs," *Journal of Academic Librarianship* 13 (May 1987): 86–92; Larry Millsap and Terry Ellen Ferl, "Search Patterns of Remote Users: An Analysis of OPAC Transacation Logs," *Information Technology & Libraries* 12 (Sept. 1993): 335.

16. Markey, *Subject Searching in Library Catalogs*, 77.

17. Ray R. Larson, "Between Scylla and Charybdis: Subject Searching in the Online Catalog," *Advances in Librarianship* 15 (1991): 180–83.

18. Rhonda N. Hunter, "Success and Failure of Patrons Searching the Online Catalog at a Large Academic Library: A Transaction Log Analysis," *RQ* 30 (spring 1991): 395.

19. Thomas A. Peters, "When Smart People Fail: An Analysis of the Transaction Log of an Online Public Access Catalog," *Journal of Academic Librarianship* 15 (Nov. 1989): 270.

20. Patricia M. Wallace, "How Do Patrons Search the Online Catalog When No One's Looking? Transaction Log Analysis and Implications for Bibliographic Instruction and System Design," *RQ* 33 (winter 1993): 247–48.

21. See, for example, Ray R. Larson, "The Decline of Subject Searching: Long-Term Trends and Patterns of Index Use in an Online Catalog," *Journal of the American Society for Information Science* 42 (Apr. 1991): 197–215; Ensor, "User Characteristics of Keyword Searching in an OPAC," 72–80.

22. Markey, *Subject Searching in Library Catalogs*, 70.

23. For example, Hsieh-Yee, "Student Use of Online Catalogs and Other Information Channels," 166.

24. For example, Karen Markey, *Research Report on the Process of Subject Searching in the Library Catalog: Final Report of the Subject Access Research Project* (Dublin, Ohio: OCLC, 1983), 31; Steinberg and Metz, "User Response to and Knowledge about Online Catalogs," 69; Frost, "Faculty Use of Subject Searching in Card and Online Catalogs," 91; Hsieh-Yee, "Student Use of Online Catalogs and Other Information Channels," 166.

25. Lori Franz, John Powell, Susan Jude, and Karen M. Drabenstott, "End-User Understanding of Subdivided Subject Headings," *Library Resources & Technical Service*, 38 (July 1994): 213.

26. Norgard et al., "The Online Catalog, 114.

27. Stephen E. Wiberley Jr. and Robert Allen Daugherty, "Users' Persistence in Scanning Lists of References," *College & Research Libraries* 49 (Mar. 1988): 152–53. In a later investigation, Wiberley, Daugherty, and James A. Danowski found that helpful ordering of retrievals seems to increase persistence to displaying 200 postings. More research is needed to corroborate this finding. (Stephen E. Wiberley Jr., Robert Allen Daugherty, and James A. Danowski, "User Persistence in Displaying Online Catalog Postings: LUIS," *Library Resources & Technical Services* 39 (July 1995): 247–68.)

28. Karen Markey, "Integrating the Machine-Readable LCSH into Online Catalogs," *Information Technology & Libraries* 7 (Sept. 1988): 300.

29. Ruth Hafter, *Academic Librarians and Cataloging Networks: Visibility, Quality Control, and Professional Status.* (Westport, Conn.: Greenwood Pr., 1986), 129.

30. See, for example, Joseph C. Harmon, "The Death of Quality Cataloging: Does It Make a Difference for Library Users? *Journal of Academic Librarianship* 22 (July 1996): 306–7.

31. Sarah E. Thomas, "Quality in Bibliographic Control," *Library Trends* 44 (winter 1996): 494.

32. Pat Oddy, *Future Libraries, Future Catalogues* (London: Library Association Publishing, 1996), 91.

33. See Andrew D. Osborn's "The Crisis in Cataloging," *Library Quarterly* 11 (Oct. 1941): 393–411, for an early discussion of the conflict.

34. Arnold Hirshon, "The Lobster Quadrille: The Future of Technical Services in a Re-Engineering World," in *The Future is Now: The Changing Face of Technical Services* (Dublin, Ohio: Ohio Computer Library Center, 1994), 17.

35. Clare B. Dunkle, "Outsourcing the Catalog Department. A Meditation Inspired by the Business and Library Literature," *Journal of Academic Librarianship* 22 (Jan. 1996): 33–43.

36. Ibid., 42.

37. Lois Buttlar and Rajinder Garcha, "Catalogers in Academic Libraries: Their Evolving and Expanding Roles," *College & Research Libraries* 59 (July 1998): 311–21.

38. Michael Gorman, "The Organization of Academic Libraries in the Light of Automation," *Advances in Library Automation and Networking* 1 (1987): 164–66.

39. Jennifer Ann Younger, "University Library Effectiveness: A Case Study of Perceived Outcomes of Structural Change" (Ph.D. diss., Univ. of Wisconsin-Madison, 1990), 78.

40. Jerry D. Campbell, "Shaking the Conceptual Foundations of Reference: A Perspective," *Reference Services Review* (winter 1992): 32–33.

41. Lisa Romero and Nancy Romero, "Original Cataloging in a Decentralized Environment: An Identification and Explanation of Errors," *Cataloging & Classification Quarterly* 15, no. 4 (1992): 47–65. The authors identified many errors that would not interfere with the user's ability to locate information.

42. John J. Reimer, "A Practitioner's View of the Education of Catalogers," *Cataloging & Classification Quarterly* 16, no. 3 (1993): 40.

43. Michael Gorman, "How Cataloging and Classification Should Be Taught," *American Libraries* 23 (Sept. 1992): 694.

44. Pauline A. Cochrane, *Improving LCSH for Use in Online Catalogs* (Littleton, Colo.: Libraries Unlimited, 1986), 13–94.

45. Sanford Berman, "Proposals for Reforms to Improve Subject Searching," in *Improving LCSH for Use in Online Catalogs*, 121–22. And also his *Prejudices and Antipathies: A Tract on the LC Subject Heads Concerning People*, 1993 ed. (Jefferson, N.C.: McFarland, 1993).

46. Michael Buckland, *Redesigning Library Services: A Manifesto*. (Chicago: ALA, 1992), 2–41.

47. Hugh C. Atkinson, "Classification in an Unclassified World," in *Classification of Library Materials: Current and Future Potential for Providing Access*, ed. Betty G. Bengtson and Janet Swan Hill (New York: Neal-Schuman, 1990), 7.

Reference:
Putting Users First

John C. Stalker

One of the apparent but often ignored truths in librarianship is that there is not just *a* patron, or just *the* patron, but there are many patrons, each of whom brings to the library a unique set of needs and an equally unique way of using library materials.[1]

Reference service is a relatively recent development in the long history of libraries. For most of that history, acquiring materials and making them available for use were the universally recognized reasons for the existence of libraries. The earliest library survey, conducted in the late eighteenth century, describes collections but does not mention any personal mediation.[2] Samuel Rothstein has traced the history of reference service in North America.[3] He shows that in its traditional form, reference is barely a century old. Although the famous *Report on Public Libraries in the United States of 1876* makes no mention at all of reference work, librarians in that significant year did recognize that users need help with the techniques of finding materials and guidance in evaluating what they found. At that year's founding conference of the American Library Association, Samuel Swett Green advocated librarian assistance to readers. In the same year, in the new periodical *Library Journal*, he published a version of his remarks in an article entitled "Personal Relations between Librarians and Readers."[4] Green realized that readers needed assistance in using the library and also recognized that personal assistance made them more inclined to support the library.

Although service to the user is the goal of all aspects of library work, the reference department or reference service is where the user is most likely to find a knowledgeable human to assist in deciphering the maze of information-finding tools and collections that comprise the contemporary academic library. In order to analyze the current state of personal assistance to users, John M. Budd has recently urged the use of "user-centered theory" in thinking about reference service. His idea is based on modern literary theory. He observes that the reader is not inherently capable of interpreting the "texts" presented by the library and that "one aspect of the reference librarian's job is to act as a mediator between the library and its catalog and the user. As such the librarian acts as an interpretive filter."[5] Taking literary theory a step further, one might attempt to "deconstruct" the reference interview. Seen in this light, the most significant aspect of the reference transaction is not the transfer of a commodity (information) from the knowledgeable librarian to the ignorant user. The most significant purpose of reference service is to empower the user. With the assistance of the reference librarian, the user learns how to decode the library's resources and the library itself, and to gain mastery of the skills needed to obtain information. Thus, users should be the center of reference activities.

Reference Service Challenged

Personal reference service, as first advocated by Samuel Green in 1876, remains as necessary as ever, and users have better service than ever before. However, reference service on the brink of the twenty-first century is faced with challenges beyond Green's imagining. During most of its first hundred years, reference service was stable. Service was provided at a centrally located desk staffed at all times by fully trained librarians. The traditional reference desk served users well who came to the reference room. Despite occasional location changes due to remodeling, reference desks tended to stay put for decades. Reference books also had an essentially fixed location. Shifting the collection might sometimes confuse and irritate users, but they could usually count on finding a reference tool where they had last used it. Catalog drawers, index volumes, and reference books could be carried about to some extent, but the work required to carry them any great distance was sufficient to ensure that the next re-shelving sweep would restore them to their proper places. Moreover, catalog information desks could be placed among the catalog cabinet, and reference desks among index tables and reference shelving. The user could find a likely source of personal assistance with ease, and the reference librarians accurately learned to identify perplexed users.

Technology has changed this situation, however. The locus of reference activity has changed from a collection of books in a fixed location to a computer screen. The question of where to go to find a reference source has become a question of how to access the tool from a terminal that can be anywhere. The user who needs to know what key to tap in order to go to the next screen of a bibliographic record may not be in the same room, building, city, or country as the person best suited to help. Although information technology has greatly enhanced libraries' ability to meet user needs, it has also placed great stress on reference librarians. Reference librarians are hard-pressed to both learn the new systems and teach the tools to baffled users.[6] When one system has been fully mastered, another one, seemingly completely different, supersedes it. More insidiously, during the short life span of each system, subtly enhanced versions appear with startling regularity. True online catalogs are hardly two decades old, but viable systems receive upgrades every year or disappear. Migration to another system is not uncommon.[7] Users and staff alike are bewildered because "we are adding to the complexity of choice in deciding which system contains the information desired, and each generation of computer-based tools, while claiming user friendliness, requires new levels of expertise for both librarian and client."[8] Reference librarians appear to suffer from burnout due to these technological changes and to the downsizing that has resulted from a decrease in library buying power.[9] A recent *Library Journal* survey shows that seven out of ten librarians believe that technology is today's greatest job concern.[10]

In response to the impact of technology on libraries, there has been a movement to "rethink" reference. Arnold Hirshon summarizes some of its proposals.[11] He divides the proposals into two categories: customer service and the technological environment. Customer service recommendations include the creation of a triage system, development of mechanisms to obtain user feedback, and well-designed user guides and good signage, including staff name tags. Needed for the technological environment are powerful workstations housed at ergonomically designed work spaces that can easily be monitored by reference librarians; a wide range of networked online indexes and abstracting services; and full-text and image databases Services and databases should be fully available at remote locations so that patrons can initiate requests there.

Customer Service

In a triage system, users with low-level needs are directed to students or paraprofessional staff;[12] only users with problems of greater difficulty are sent to a desk staffed by professionals. In some libraries, those with problems demanding deep expertise for solution go to a consultation office. The triage system may utilize an information desk situated around the online catalog and staffed by students or other nonprofessional workers.[13] In this scenario, information desk workers assist patrons in using the catalog and answer ready reference questions but refer all other questions to a reference librarian at a reference department. In a more radical variation, the reference desk is eliminated entirely and replaced by a research consultation office.[14] Ironically, even when libraries do not establish a triage system, library users informally establish one. They are as likely to ask for help from a circulation clerk or a student assistant as a reference librarian.

Although triage can free librarians to concentrate on more serious reference questions, the creation of a triage system may not in and of itself create good reference service. Users rightly balk at repeated referrals, and in both formal and informal triage, staff training is critical. The staff in all public service areas need to be trained in how and when to make referrals. Users need to perceive that the referral will benefit them. To make the triage process work, the user must have a sense of personal assistance. Research has shown that the nearby presence of a librarian available for consultation improves the success rate of staff working in a triage system.[15]

An increasing body of research has begun to tell reference librarians more about their users both collectively and in selected groups. User studies disclose the importance of the personal characteristics of librarians, such as approachability and friendliness.[16] Studies of scholarly communication provide revealing insights into the use, often the lack of use, of reference service by the scholarly community. In-house feedback from suggestion boxes, surveys, and focus groups can help librarians understand their users better. It is, however, important to recognize that many library users are reluctant to reveal problems with reference service: in some cases, they do not know that they have problems, and in other cases, they are unaware that their problems can be solved.

Technology now provides another way to learn in depth about users. Automated systems create transaction logs that furnish reference staff with a record (available for later analysis) of every keystroke the user makes.[17] The researcher can study users without standing clipboard in hand at their elbows, thereby influencing their behavior. This unobtrusive data-gathering allows librarians to discover what users are doing and to modify systems to help them.

Signage and user guides both off- and online are essential parts of good reference service. Locally created aids should be comprehensible to users. Brochures and handouts should be clear, concise, and understandable. Personal interactions between reference librarians and users can evaluate such aids. A brochure or computer screen that frequently needs explanation has questionable value and is probably flawed. Representation of locations by cryptic abbreviations may make efficient use of system resources, but it needlessly perplexes patrons. In general, the reference department should serve as the user's advocate for standards of intelligent design and good writing. Reference librarians have an obligation to inform database developers and vendors of user needs and preferences.

Respecting Differences among Users

Although the "customer service" recommendations of the "rethinking reference" movement are important, the first step in putting users at the center is to realize that they have different needs and that even the same user's needs vary with time and circumstance. Differences go beyond divisions in status, such as undergraduates, graduate students, and faculty. Recent education research has highlighted the importance of learning styles.[18] Learning style differences affect not only the way people use libraries, but also the way they learn to use them. Not every user wants personal assistance, but then again, not every user wants to be independent. The excellent reference librarian is a perceptive judge of a user's personal style, in addition to having traditional reference skills. When users come to an impasse and cannot continue without personal assistance, they deserve access to a reference librarian who can assess and meet their needs.

For a user, an impasse may arise at any point in the information-seeking process. Each user who begins to work in a particular library or who starts research in a previously unfamiliar area faces myriad minor problems. Each library has its own physical configuration to decipher. Where are the terminals, and to what do they allow access? Where are current periodicals, bound periodicals, books, and copiers? How does the user find out whether this library has a copy of a given item? The precise tool required to find materials of a certain type or date varies from library to library. For example, some periodical indexes may be included in the online catalog; some may require consecutive searches, whereas others afford simultaneous searching; location and availability appear immediately in some databases but in others require separate searches. Each online system reflects a heritage of shifting local practices that affect the location and presentation of information.

Successive users may appear with essentially the same set of questions. When many students are working on the same assignment, questions recur and may at any given time comprise the majority of interactions. Many of these questions are easily answered in a short time without a great depth of knowledge, but the reference librarian must avoid the unwarranted conclusion that the users are ignorant. Such an attitude will be communicated to them and hinder their successful use of the library. User-centered service requires empathy and patience. Librarians should remember their own confusion during the first day on the job in any library. Also (and more difficult), they should recognize that the user may have a style of coping with initial confusion that may well differ from their own. For example, some users and librarians love signs and maps, others do not even notice them.

After a period of adjustment to the particularities of a library, some users can satisfy their needs most of the time without further interaction. This ability to function independently is related to learning style and personal preferences. The way patrons use computerized systems highlights differences in their learning styles.[19] Some prefer graphics and others text.[20] There is clear evidence that matching learning styles to presentation enhances learning.[21]

The Technological Environment

The quality and amount of information technology available are often determined by financial resources rather than by the careful planning of the library staff. However, librarians in general, and reference librarians in particular, play an important role in making the technology accessible to users. Users do not come any better equipped to understand the new electronic resources than they did the older printed sources. As learning takes place, users may require less human intervention. An important step in putting users first is to make the library's new technology as usable as possible without assistance. Michael Gorman has proposed as an ideal, a library in which personal assistance and training are not required.[22] Not every user can learn without personal intervention, but some users prefer to use computerized systems without assistance. For them especially, but for other users too, well-designed help screens and clearly written brochures will be important aids. Users who prefer to work independently can also benefit from expert systems, artificial intelligence, and computer-aided instruction.[23]

Although help from online and printed sources is important, assistance from another person can be just as significant. Some users, whether because of personality or learning style, will be unreceptive to electronic assistance. Jennifer Mendelsohn has found that "research on in-person help supports the idea that users need and want human help even more than printed online help."[24] Thus, no matter how well they prepare online or printed help, reference librarians still need to provide personal assistance to users of automated systems. They will also be called upon to help users who only seek personal assistance when they are stymied.

Changes in searching for periodical articles illustrate how technology can create the illusion that users no longer need assistance. In the past, finding a relevant article was often a time-consuming, tedious, and irritating process. The user first had to identify the appropriate abstracts and indexes and then determine the correct subject headings for the topic. Next followed consulting numerous index volumes; accumulating a list of citations; checking the serials catalog or printed list of periodicals; finding bound volumes in the stacks; and consulting union lists to determine the location of others in order to obtain the remainder later through interlibrary loan. Furthermore, many indexes required double lookup or checking lists of abbreviations in the frontmatter to complete citations.

A present-day search for periodical articles can be quite different. The user sits at a terminal, hits a few keys to access the appropriate database, and types a few keywords to retrieve relevant citations. The citations may indicate whether the local collection contains copies; or better still, a function key retrieves the full text of the articles from a remote site. Although finding relevant periodical articles may not have achieved this level in every library, progress in the past couple of years makes this scenario increasingly prevalent and perhaps even expected by many users. Nevertheless, there may be many situations where users will need human assistance. Users cannot always determine which database is best for a particular subject. For some subjects, no satisfactory database may exist, and many subjects still require checking paper indexes for a thorough search. Subject terminology varies from database to database, and some databases require the use of sophisticated thesauri for true success. Databases proliferate but also occasionally disappear because either the producer no long supplies them or the cost to the institution is prohibitive. Mechanisms for finding, limiting, displaying, and printing are inconsistent across databases, sometimes even within a single database. The same database may be available in a given library from different vendors who use different protocols. All of these factors—the degree of difficulty, the variation in database design, and the ignorance of the user—make personal intervention by a knowledgeable librarian as important today as in the precomputer era.

A generation ago, library building consultants stressed that good library design meant that the user, upon entering the library, be presented with the "keys" to the library; that is, the user should be able to see and identify the catalog, the circulation desk, and the reference desk.[25] Now that users need not physically visit a library building to use library resources, equivalent keys must be found to unlock those resources for the remote user. The underlying design principle remains the same. The door to the library may now be a computer screen and that door must be a window through which the user can see the "keys" to library collections. E-mail is a logical window, rather straightforward to set up,[26] and is already used by many libraries.[27] A recent study suggests that e-mail users prefer this mode to in-person assistance by a proportion of three to two.[28] Users who enter the library through a network from their homes or offices probably already have access to e-mail, but the appropriate library e-mail address must be available. Luckily, the library's Web home page and the initial screen of the library's online system offer logical places for information on the reference department's e-mail capabilities.

Reference using electronic mail is almost the same as traditional mail or telephone reference, and e-mail has the same advantages and limitations. These limitations are serious. The user is removed from the source of assistance. Reference interviews are difficult to conduct in person. E-mail does not allow as much interaction as face-to-face conversation. With e-mail, users with technical sophistication and superior typing skills are privileged over their less accomplished colleagues. Electronic mail works best for clearly definable problems with clearly expressible answers. If, as predicted, e-mail inquiries progress from ready reference questions to more substantive questions, electronic assistance will need to become less like correspondence and more like conversation.[29] Telecommunication technology allows real-time transmission of full-motion video over telephone lines. By using full-motion video, perhaps the workstation screen can then become a true window to personal reference assistance. Ideally, the system will be programmed to detect user difficulty in finding assistance. The user can then be prompted, without unnecessary intrusion, to open the reference desk help window and be offered the opportunity to contact a virtual reference desk with a real reference librarian. Traditional staffing problems of telephone and walk-up reference assistance will remain the same. Queuing theory predicts how often users will receive a busy signal, how long they will wait for a callback, and how many will be in line at the desk. Electronic pathways have their own queues. Keeping the frustration at an acceptable level remains as much a staffing problem as a technological puzzle.

The Internet, especially in the form of the World Wide Web, appears destined to alter the traditional notion of a library and to change the scope and nature of reference assistance.[30] Various powerful reference tools reside only in Cyberspace.[31] Once time-consuming tasks such as constructing a legislative history for a bill under current consideration, finding the address (e-mail or otherwise) of a faculty member at a foreign university, or providing weather data for Montana can be done in an instant—provided one can find the appropriate Internet resource.

Internet browsers such as Netscape and Explorer leverage computer technology to make electronic resources more accessible to nonexperts. Selecting a link on a home page can lead to usable information. Browsers employ client–server technology. The browser computer has the necessary software to get information from a remote computer. For example, a server at Virginia has information about electronic text projects.[32] Moreover, the Virginia software is sufficiently sophisticated that it both searches this index and retrieves texts so identified that are stored on computers at other institutions. For instance, a user at a small college in Alaska can retrieve a text located on a server in Florida. The user in Alaska does not need to know how exactly all of this is accomplished. The text seemingly appears miraculously on the screen. Perhaps even the digitized image of the original manuscript may be available.

Such wonders of technology will become increasingly commonplace, but that does not mean they are without problems. For one, retrieving a given text or item of information on a computer does not guarantee that it is authoritative and reliable. Even if librarians are not experts about, say, textual criticism or legislative history, they must preserve their traditional role of saying "caveat emptor." Second, few objects in Cyberspace stay put. IP addresses change as servers change. Third, publishers and other information providers offer free access as a means of testing commercial viability and attracting customers; then they limit access to those who pay. Home page designs change as server software incorporates more functionality; client browsers in turn need updating to take advantage of the new capabilities. The improvements are frequently substantial but have unexpected consequences, and they usually demand adjustments by the user.

Conclusion

This is a time to go back to first principles.[33] Reference involves two aspects: (1) supplying information from sources the library owns or to which it provides access; and (2) working with the user as a person (i.e., managing the interpersonal aspects of the reference encounter). Reference librarians are essentially mediators who work on behalf of users.[34] In their role as mediators, they must know the sources that contain the information users need, and they must be up to date with new information technology. This requires a commitment to learning on their part, but it also demands an institutional commitment to adequate training and continuing education. At the same time, reference librarians must concentrate on the underlying principle of personal assistance with which Green inaugurated traditional reference librarianship. Drawing, like Budd, from modern communication theory, Marie L. Radford writes: "Surrounded by texts, indexing systems, and information technologies of all kinds, the encounter between reference librarian and the user represents the human interface between the library's knowledge and the library user's need for information."[35] In her terms, the "relational" as much as or more than the content dimensions of the encounter are the true measure of success. By concentrating on the relational dimensions, librarians will be alert and sensitive to the unique needs of each individual user. They will provide the personalized service that will give users the information and attention they need. Users will value the librarian's work and support the library's future efforts to help them.

Notes

1. Hugh C. Atkinson, "Classification in an Unclassified World," in *Classification of Library Materials: Current and Future Potential for Providing Access,* ed. Betty G. Bengtson and Janet Swan Hill (New York: Neal-Schuman, 1990), p.7.

2. Thomas D. Walker, "The First Use of a Library Questionnaire: Adalbert Blumenschein's Eighteenth-Century Study of European Libraries," *Library & Information Science Research* 16 (winter 1994): 59–66.

3. Samuel Rothstein, "The Development of the Concept of Reference Service in American Libraries, 1850–1900," *Library Quarterly* 23 (Jan. 1953): 1–15. A more recent discussion can be found in the special issue "Developing Readers' Advisory Services: Concepts and Commitments," ed. Kathleen de la Pena McCook and Gary O. Rolstad, *Collection Building* 12, nos. 3–4 (1993).

4. Samuel Swett Green, "Personal Relations between Librarians and Readers," *Library Journal* (Oct. 1876): 74–81.

5. John M. Budd, "User-Centered Thinking: Lessons from Reader-Centered Theory," *RQ* 34 (summer 1995): 487–96.

6. Mara R. Saule, "User Instruction Issues for Databases in the Humanities," *Library Trends* 40 (spring 1992): 596–613; and Linda J. Piele, "Reference Services and Staff Training for Patron-Use Software," *Library Trends* 40 (summer 1991): 97–119.

7. Ibid, 97–119; Saule, "User Instruction Issues," 596–613.

8. Janice Simmons-Welburn, "New Technologies and Reference Services," *RQ* 33 (fall 1993): 16–19.

9. Ron Blazek and Darlene Ann Parrish, "Burnout and Public Services: The Periodical Literature of Librarianship in the Eighties," *RQ* 32 (fall 1992): 48–59.

10. "Technology Is Dramatically Changing the Way Librarians Work," *Library Journal* 119 (Nov. 1, 1994): 49.

11. Arnold Hirshon, "Running with the Red Queen: Breaking New Habits to Survive in the Virtual World," *Advances in Librarianship* 20 (1996): 4–5.

12. Larry Oberg has made provocative and stimulating remarks on the role of paraprofessionals in "The Emergence of the Paraprofessional in Academic Libraries: Perceptions and Realities," *College & Research Libraries* 53 (Mar. 1992): 99–112; and his "Reference Services in an On-line Environment: Some Implications for Staffing," in *Rethinking Reference in Academic Libraries*, ed. Anne Grodzins Lipow (Berkeley, Calif.: Library Solutions Pr., 1993), 71–76. Carol Hammond, "Information and Research Support Services: The Reference Librarian and the Information Paraprofessional," *Reference Librarian*, no. 37 (1992): 91–104, elicited Mr. Oberg's "Response," *Reference Librarian*, no. 37 (1992): 105–7.

13. Beth S. Woodard, "The Effectiveness of an Information Desk Staffed by Graduate Students and Nonprofessionals," *College & Research Libraries* 50 (July 1989): 455–67.

14. Virginia Massey-Burzio, "Reference Encounters of a Different Kind: A Symposium," *Journal of Academic Librarianship* 18 (Nov. 1992): 276–80.

15. Marjorie E. Murfin and Charles A. Bunge, "Paraprofessionals at the Reference Desk," *Journal of Academic Librarianship* 14 (Mar. 1988): 14.

16. For a summary of research about the personal characteristics of librarians, see Ellen D. Sutton and Leslie Edmonds Holt, "The Reference Interview," in *Reference and Information Services: An Introduction,* ed. Richard E. Bopp and Linda C. Smith (Englewood, Colo.: Libraries Unlimited, 1995), 38–39.

17. Barbara M. Wildemuth, Ruth De Bliek, and Shaoyi S. He, "Search Moves Made by Novice End Users," *ASIS '92: Proceedings of the 55th ASIS Annual Meeting.* (Medford, New Jersey: Learned Information, 1992), 154–61.

18. Rita Staford Dunn, et al., "Survey of Research on Learning Styles," *Educational Leadership* 46 (Mar. 1989): 50–58.

19. Gene Geisert, et al. "Reading, Learning Styles, and Computers," *Journal of Reading, Writing, & Learning Disabilities International* 6, (July–Sept.1990): 297–305.

20. Richard Riding and Graeme Douglas, "The Effect of Cognitive Style and Mode of Presentation on Learning Performance," *British Journal of Educational Psychology* 63, no. 2 (1993): 297–307.

21. Helen L. Carlson, "Learning Style and Program Design in Interactive Multimedia," *Educational Technology Research & Development* 39, no. 3 (1991): 41–48; Valerie J. Shute, "A Comparison of Learning Environments: All That Glitters," in *Computers as Cognitive Tools,* ed. Susanne P. Lajoie and Sharon J. Derry (Hillsdale, N.J.: Lawrence Erlbaum Associates, 1993), 47–73.

22. Michael Gorman, "Send for a Child of Four: Or, Creating the BI-less Academic Library," *Library Trends* (winter 1991): 354–62.

23. Ralph Alberico and H. Mary Micco, *Expert Systems for Reference and Information Retrieval* (Westport, Conn.: Meckler, 1990); Anne Morris, *The Application of Expert Systems in Libraries and Information Centres* (London and New York: Bowker-Saur, 1992).

24. Jennifer Mendelsohn, "Human Help at OPAC Terminals Is User Friendly: A Preliminary Study," *RQ* 34 (winter 1994): 185.

25. Keyes D. Metcalf, *Planning Academic and Research Library Buildings* (New York: McGraw-Hill, 1965).

26. Patrick R. Dewey, *E-MAIL for Libraries* (Westport, Conn.: Meckler, 1989).

27. Julie M.Still and Frank M.Campbell, "Librarian in a Box: The Use of Electronic Mail for Reference," *Reference Services Review* 21 (1993): 15–18.

28. Lara Bushallow-Wilbur, Gemma S. DeVinney, and Fritz Whitcomb, "Electronic Mail Reference Service: A Study," *RQ* 35 (spring 1996): 359–63.

29. Eileen G. Abels, "The E-mail Reference Interview," *RQ* 35 (spring 1996): 345–58.

30. Steve Mitchell and Margaret T. Mooney, "INFOMINE—A Model Web-Based Academic Virtual Library," *Information Technology & Libraries* 15 (Mar. 1996): 20–25.

31. Don Lanier and Walter Wilkins, "Ready Reference via the Internet," *RQ* 33 (spring 1994): 359–68; Scott A. Mellendorf, "Pounding the Pavement with Purpose: Utilizing the Information Superhighway for Daily Work Tasks," *RQ* 35 (winter 1995): 231–35.

32. David M. Seaman, "A Library and Apparatus of Every Kind: The Electronic Text Center at the University of Virginia," *Information Technology & Libraries* 13 (Mar. 1994): 15–19.

33. Claudette S. Hagle, "Back to Basics: Recommitment to Patron's Information Needs," *Reference Librarian*, no. 37 (1992): 37–48.

34. Arthur W. Hafner and Valerie M. Camarigg, "The Librarian as Mediator," *Reference Librarian*, no. 37 (1992): 3–22.

35. Marie L. Radford, "Communication Theory Applied to the Reference Encounter: An Analysis of Critical Incidents," *Library Quarterly* 66 (Apr. 1996): 123–37.

Interlibrary Services from Both Sides of the Desk

Richard M. Dougherty and Juliet Williams

> There are three principles which I think should be applied
> to all resource sharing: (1) That it should be quick, (2) that
> the sharing should be integral to internal use, and (3) lastly,
> the sharing process should enhance the local library service,
> not be a supplement to it.[1]

The business of interlibrary loan (ILL) in academic libraries currently demands attention. Increasing use by patrons, rising costs,
staff shortages, and the growing bibliographical access to information
have all contributed to the stress interlibrary units are currently experiencing. Such pressures are forcing ILL librarians to take a harder
look at current procedures in an effort to streamline operations and
reduce costs. Most libraries now utilize telecommunications such
as RLIN and OCLC to receive and transmit ILL requests. The
electronically based procedures speed up parts of the process, just
as public access to databases stimulates more users to submit requests. Of course, the increasing volume only adds to the levels of
staff stress.

Recent growth in ILL traffic prompts questions such as: Are
current innovations in ILL increasing workloads without addressing
cost issues or easing the burdens on staff? Will the new capabilities
enable the ILL department to keep pace with the new demands?

Ultimately, and most important, do these improvements increase the level of service offered to users? That is, does more service necessarily translate into better service?

In exploring these issues, this chapter reviews the services that are typically available to users, including a picture of how a transaction might appear from the user's perspective. The chapter examines how costs, the proliferation of databases, and procedural complexities have impacted traditional services. Several recent developments, including multilibrary networks and the use of e-mail, are described. The paper also raises the vexing issue of how to manage growth "with less money" or "with fewer resources." Finally, a user-oriented service model is presented through the eyes of a user. The authors assume that libraries are in the midst of a paradigm shift that will ultimately transform library services and how they are delivered.

Interlibrary Loan: A User's Perspective

A library might believe its current ILL services are user oriented, but from the user's perspective, ILL services might appear to be overly bu-reaucratic, complicated, and unpredictable.[2] Our user is Sean Thompson. He is a graduate student who has been using PsycInfo to gather information for a seminar term paper. His search turns up a number of citations to articles that appear relevant to his work. After checking the university library's OPAC, Sean learns that the library owns all of the journal volumes cited but one, and that volume contains an article which appears to be relevant to Sean's topic. The OPAC has displayed a message that the journal can be requested through interlibrary loan and that assistance should be sought at the reference desk. Sean takes the printout of citations to the reference desk and informs a reference staff person (librarian or not, Sean does not know; Sean also does not know the name of the person who is assisting him). The reference staff member hands an ILL form to Sean and marks the areas to be filled out. As Sean copies the information on the printout to the form, the staff member answers another user's question. Then Sean hands the form to the reference staff member and asks, "How long will it take?" The reference worker answers, "Anywhere from five days to six weeks. We'll let you know when it arrives." Sean's paper is due next week, but the reference person has already begun to answer another user's question so Sean leaves the reference desk, deciding to trust fate that this mystical bureaucracy will churn his request through its system and spit out the article in time. Sean wonders if checking the "rush" box on the form would have ensured that the article would arrive on time.

Sean is not far off in deciding to trust fate, for, essentially, the library has also made a similar decision. By not interviewing Sean more extensively, important facts about his need for the journal article were never determined. Might those other articles, available in the library, give sufficient information for Sean to write the paper? Perhaps Sean had not looked carefully enough at the article title or the abstract and had not realized that the article was actually about a subject irrelevant to the topic of his paper. What if Sean had checked the rush box but did not meet the qualifications for a rushed request? Perhaps Sean had transposed two numbers in copying the citation onto the ILL form. Or perhaps Sean had not investigated the holdings records on the OPAC thoroughly enough and, in fact, the library does own that volume. Many of these questions could have been resolved with a more extensive interview and citation verification by the reference staff person. Without such an interview, the library places the burden for answering such questions on the ILL department after Sean is no longer immediately available to query. ILL staff must now either take the time to check the library's holdings and inform Sean by mail or telephone of the article's availability in the library (if that is the case), check with Sean to verify data, or proceed on the assumption that the information Sean provided is correct.

Sean's experience is certainly not atypical. Many transactions must be worked out without the benefit of face-to-face user–library staff interaction. But from Sean's point of view, is such a transaction really, to use the language made popular by C. Edwards Demming, "customer oriented"?

Of course, ILL has changed dramatically in recent years as supporting technologies have become available and demands for service and costs of operation have rocketed upward. Before looking at ways to improve services, it seems useful to briefly review some of the pressures under which ILL operates.

Operational Pressures
Costs

Operating under the assumption that users actually need an article they request, and when appropriate, that users need the article to be rushed, adds costs to a service that is already expensive. The white paper *Maximizing Access, Minimizing Cost,* by Shirley K. Baker and Mary E. Jackson, reports that the cost of borrowing an item has risen from $7.61 in 1971 to $19 in 1993, and lending costs have increased from $5.82 to $11 during the same period.[3] The costs represent those incurred for literal borrowing and lending of an item, such as a monograph, a journal volume, a film, etc., but do not reflect equipment and added electronic transmission charges associated with document delivery.

In 1990, Mary Jackson's ILL department at the University of Pennsylvania conducted a cost survey of its own operation that included costs incurred from faxing articles, using a statewide delivery system or UPS or U.S. mail, as well as photocopying, invoicing, and shipping. The survey found that the per-title borrowing costs for the university averaged $17.83 and that per-title lending cost $14.93.[4] Although these figures generally fall in the same range as strictly ILL-associated costs, the costs for document delivery may have increased in three years. Moreover, as libraries utilize newer technologies, such as RLG'S ARIEL, that offer greater transmission capacities but which are also more costly to acquire and maintain, at some point, lending libraries may begin to expect borrowing libraries to reimburse them for the additional expenses.

Rising per-title costs are compounded by the enormous growth in ILL traffic in recent years. Baker and Jackson's paper reports that lending by ARL (Association of Research Libraries) increased 52 percent from 1981 to 1992 , and borrowing increased 108 percent.[5] Data analyzed by Kendon Stubbs in 1992 suggest this increase in ILL use may be due to two factors. From 1986 to 1992 at ARL libraries, the number of serial titles purchased declined by two percent and the number of monograph volumes purchased decreased by 15 percent. At the same time, the number of teaching faculty rose (16 %), as did graduate students (11 %) and total students (10 %). In short, although the number of new titles available decreased, the number of potential users increased. Decreases in available titles coupled with increases in potential users may be the two significant factors that drove ILL borrowing up 47 percent and ILL lending up 45 percent during those six years.[6]

Electronic Bibliographic Databases

An additional factor that has affected the use of interlibrary loan is the increase in the number of electronic bibliographic databases available to users. CD-ROMs, remote online databases (those available through vendors such as Wilson, for example), and the Internet all provide users with more references to articles, journals, and monographs than any individual library could ever be expected to own. References to articles, of course, do not provide the article itself; more electronic bibliographic databases do not ensure greater access to information but function only as the first step in providing the user with the desired information.

The second step involves locating the referenced item and in helping the user find that item. More and more, helping the user find the item means providing interlibrary services. At Texas A&M University, Suzanne D. Gyeszly, collection development coordinator, kept statistics to chart the effects of placing three Wilson periodical indexes online. The statistics showed a 29.1 percent increase in the number of interlibrary service requests and a 45.1 percent increase in the number of patrons making the requests. Requests for articles indexed in the *Applied Science and Technology Index* alone increased by 350 percent. Based on that survey, the library decided to cancel paper copy subscriptions of the indexes in order to add more Wilson indexes to the online system and to expand interlibrary service eligibility to include undergraduates who previously had needed the permission of an instructor to place an ILL request. Gyeszly concludes that "the move in the direction of increased access means the increased importance of the Interlibrary Loan Services in bridging the gap between access and availability."[7] Electronic bibliographic databases only go halfway in helping users access information, and given the fact that libraries cannot purchase everything, interlibrary services are being used to complete the job.

Complicated Procedures

Although electronic bibliographic databases are becoming more available and easier for users to search, the method of delivering articles identified through them is not yet as quick and easy. Sean located references to pertinent articles in an afternoon, but he will have to wait at least a few days before the interlibrary loan department can deliver the requested article.

Even though more ILL departments in academic libraries are using electronic tools to speed up interlibrary transactions, quite often delivery of an item gets delayed as it moves through the ILL process. The fault does not stem from the capability of electronic networks to transmit requests and responses between libraries, nor in the capabilities of departmental staff. The fault can be traced to the underlying handling procedures[8] (e.g., repeating a shelf search when an item is not located the first time it is searched or a poorly organized request tracking system).

Operating in a telecommunications environment can add a layer of complexity when local and network procedures are poorly integrated. If an ILL department retains the initial paper form filled out by the user, or generates printouts in addition to the department's files stored on a hard drive, the department has created two trails to be maintained—a printed one and a digital one. Electronic networks and record-keeping activities should be implemented not as a parallel to pre-existing operations but as a replacement for activities performed less efficiently by hand. The greater the procedural inefficiency, the more work staff will have to do, and the longer users may have to wait.

Implementing electronic networks efficiently also requires that departments respect the rules of the network. For example, if a library's ILL department receives a request over OCLC for an item it cannot fill, the department should respond in a timely manner that the request cannot be filled so that it can be forwarded to the next potential lending institution.[9] Failing to respond to requests as a means of decreasing a department's workload neither improves the department's procedures nor enables the staff to increase its efficiency; such a practice merely ignores the real problems. From the users' perspective, such behavior only lengthens the wait time. Should such delays occur, as with Sean's request, he could have waited as long as twenty days before he learned whether a library could fill his request. Again, the fault here lies not with the staff or with OCLC's capabilities but with other departments' failures to follow network policies. Such a practice, if known to Sean, certainly would not instill in him a feeling of confidence that he will obtain the article he needs before his paper is due.

Short-term Remedies

For many of the reasons just cited, most libraries would benefit from a study of their existing procedures that aimed to streamline them. In initiating such projects, interlibrary managers could benefit from the advice of W. Edwards Deming and others in the business management field who stress total quality management (TQM). Among some of the general suggestions to managers are those that urge them to re-evaluate and change their current methods so that the overall process is made more efficient and the staff become more productive. These processes could be improved by eliminating rework and investing more authority in staff members who are therefore empowered and have a greater personal interest in their work.[10] In *Total Quality Management in Libraries*, Tom Whitehall suggests some general goals for ILL departments, in the context of TQM:

> It should be established that the client still needs the item on its arrival. Materials should be supplied three weeks from the request; 50 percent of material requested should be supplied in two weeks and 85 percent within three weeks from the date of request. Users should be informed about any delay in supplying materials ordered from another source.[11]

Whitehall suggests these goals as indicators of quality service in providing interlibrary lending and borrowing services to users. Whether these specific turnaround times and elements of interlibrary services are actually indicators of quality in the eyes of a user is open to debate. Although faster service is more appealing to users, faster service may not always equal better service. Generally speaking, the more communication with the user, the better the service is likely to be.

In an attempt to help libraries develop efficient ILL departments that do provide efficient, high-quality service to users, Baker and Jackson, in *Maximizing Access, Minimizing Costs* envision an ideal interlibrary system with particular, efficient, and cost-effective features. One of the recommendations in the white paper is that local online catalogs be designed to allow a user to search for items owned locally, and if the desired items are not locally available, to search remote suppliers and to request items from those suppliers. When catalogs capture the user's request, billing and management information will also be created.[12]

In other words, Baker and Jackson suggest that libraries create a system that is capable of handling all aspects of the interlibrary transaction: search, request, delivery, and departmental record-keeping. Such a system would cut down the potential for errors in transcribing a request from a printout to an ILL form, allow users to choose among libraries and commercial suppliers; and would lessen the chances that a department would keep two trails of records. This system would also allow the user to have more control of the process.

Even if one could create the ideal system, procedural improvements alone will not resolve all the existing problems. There are also several fundamental policy issues that must be dealt with. For example, although the ideal system would allow users to initiate their own requests for materials through ILL, does not necessarily enable users to make informed choices. Would users request interlibrary services indiscriminately and at great cost to the institution? How would a user know how long it should take for the request to be filled? Would the user know that commercial suppliers are available, the differences among them, and the costs that would be assessed? Would there be any system-imposed provisions that would restrain a user from petitioning several different suppliers for the same item? Would libraries be put in the position of filling requests that users would never retrieve? Before it will be possible to create a truly user-oriented service, one must first resolve such issues by pilot testing and cost-benefit analysis.

Recent Developments
In recent years, a variety of innovations have been introduced to im-

prove the efficiency of library operations and the quality of library service. The use of fax and even more recently the use of the Internet to transmit nonreturnable loans has mushroomed, speeding up the delivery of these articles. Some libraries now permit users to submit requests via e-mail. If Sean works at home and his computer is linked to the campus network, this added feature could be a real time-saver. But of probably greater interest to Sean has been the development of multilibrary networks that not only expand the resources available to him but, as in the case of ILLINET and OhioLINK, possess the potential of greatly reducing the traditional headaches associated with securing materials from other libraries. Some of these developments are briefly discussed in the following sections.

E-mail

Amy Chang, coordinator for interlibrary loan at Texas Tech, described the electronic mail system developed by her staff.[13] This system allows users to request materials through their e-mail accounts. After entering "ILL" as an option, the user is asked to complete a short identification form and as many request forms as necessary. Pull-up instructions for assistance in filling out the forms are available. The user may also choose a "Questions-and-Answers" menu to find information such as How long will it take? and How much will it cost? The user may then return to the main menu or log off. After the user exits the system, the requests are forwarded to the ILL department for handling.

The e-mail request capability was designed in response to an in-house study that had identified as problems "the inconvenience and the time-consuming process of communicating between the staff and the patron."[14] Communicating via e-mail was seen as a desirable solution because the system allows users to request materials at their convenience and also allows staff to communicate directly with users over a reliable system. Chang discussed the initial construction and implementation of the system but did not indicate how the use of e-mail has affected the ILL department. Whether e-mail communication has actually eased staff workload is not discussed, nor is the effect that the use of e-mail may have on other forms of communication with users. Do fewer users request materials by mail or phone now that they have the option of using their e-mail accounts? Although Chang does not indicate whether the number of requests increased as a result of the new option, given the convenience of requesting materials from a remote location at any time of day or night, Texas Tech's ILL department will ultimately experience increased usage.

Although e-mail allows for direct and fast communication, the depth of communication that can take place is limited. Whether this limitation is significant enough to lower the overall quality of service is not known. From the user's perspective, the verdict is clear: e-mail offers an additional service option. From a library staff's perspective, the verdict might not be so clear because the use of e-mail might result in additional work if the new procedures are not carefully crafted to avoid additional steps in processing requests (e.g., transcribing data from one format to another). Of course, the next step will be to enhance digital communications of ILL information through the Web. Such a network is already emerging rapidly.

Multiple-Library Networks

Although the e-mail request option allows users to telecommunicate their interlibrary requests to library staff, at the same time libraries have begun to use telecommunications networks for communicating among themselves. Such systems have become quite common in recent years. One well-known and effective multiple-library network is located in Minnesota.

The Minnesota State University System (MSUS) of 53 state university, community college, private college, and state agency libraries is linked by the Project for Automated Library Systems (PALS).[15] The PALS network serves as an online catalog to assist functions of circulation, acquisitions, and serials control within each of the libraries. PALS allows libraries to update and maintain their own holdings and also to view the records of other member libraries.

Interlibrary loan is one feature of the PALS network. Libraries can use the PALS system to create, send, receive, and track ILL requests. Through this network, libraries have the option of contacting each other directly to fill ILL requests, or they can route the request to an ILL center, known as MINITEX. This network is publicly supported by a grant from the Minnesota state legislature and consists of academic, public, state agency, and special libraries.[16] When

MINITEX receives an ILL request, staff first search the collections of the University of Minnesota, Twin Cities Campus Libraries, and other libraries in the Twin Cities. If the appropriate item is located at one of these institutions, MINITEX will lend or photocopy it and deliver it to the requesting library. If the item is not available from those institutions, MINITEX will electronically refer the request to libraries throughout Minnesota and the Dakotas. MINITEX may also forward the request to libraries in Wisconsin, the Illinois State Library, the Library of Congress, or the British Library Document Supply Center, to single out but a few of the available options.

In addition to greatly increasing the pool of resources available to users such as Sean, these networks enable libraries to simplify aspects of processing operations. For example, the ILL department at Bemidji State University reports that verification of the requests is made easier with the PALS system, that tracking problem requests is simplified, and that more detailed lending and borrowing statistics are compiled and readily available to staff.[17]

Interlibrary Loan Becomes Circulation
Even more extensive alterations to the traditional interlibrary process have been made in Illinois and Ohio.[18] Librarians in both states use a system of electronic networks that allow materials to be requested directly by the user, rather than through the user's local interlibrary loan office. The two networks are ILLINET Online, which began in the 1980s, and OhioLINK, which became operational in 1992.

ILLINET Online grew to its current organizational form from the University of Illinois's Library Computing System (LCS). ILLINET Online became operational in 1980, linking through a shared circulation system the online catalogs of fifteen libraries, including the University of Illinois.[19] To foster resource-sharing among libraries, LCS was expanded to include catalog records of a total of eight hundred libraries and to allow 2,600 Illinois libraries to access ILLINET Online. At the core of the system are forty-five libraries that are members of the Illinois Library Computer System Organization (ILCSO). Among the ILCSO members are the libraries of Illinois's state-supported universities, twenty-six private colleges and universities, four community colleges, the Illinois State Library, and one state-supported high school for math and the sciences. These forty-five libraries use the system for their local operations, resource-sharing, and interlibrary circulation. Any of the 2,600 libraries may use ILLINET Online for interlibrary services. Although the ILCSO libraries do not engage in document delivery service through circulation services, the system does utilize the services of Carl UnCover. In addition, plans are in the works to provide access to IAC's Academic Index and ASAP over the Internet, which would allow access to full-text articles of 200 journal titles.

ILLINET Online moves beyond the traditional concept of interlibrary lending in the processes available through the ILCSO libraries. Any authorized users at terminals connected to the system can serve themselves in requesting materials from other libraries. This means that Sean may borrow books from any terminal in any member library. He charges the item to his student identification number. His charge initiates a delivery request at the holding library, where staff fill Sean's request. In effect, then, the transaction becomes not an interlibrary loan but a circulation activity.[20] The item is delivered to Sean's library using a statewide service known as the Intersystem Library Delivery Service (ILDS). This service connects the local delivery systems.[21]

Following Illinois's lead, Ohio developed a similar system, OhioLINK.[22] OhioLINK's central catalog includes the holdings records of the libraries at seventeen public universities, all two-year institutions of higher education, eleven private colleges, and the State Library of Ohio.[23] In addition, OhioLINK provides access to bibliographic databases including the full-text versions of a wide range of research databases, and offers a Web gateway to the Internet. The system allows users at any of the libraries to initiate interlibrary requests from any of the other member institutions. In general, the system functions in much the same way as ILLINET Online.

Even though OhioLINK and ILLINET Online promote resource-sharing to a level never before realized, these new service models also raise a number of questions and concerns. With such tremendous increases in circulation activity and plans to expand the systems to include more libraries, will the staff of member libraries reach a burnout stage? Can the additional workloads and costs be managed?

Systems such as ILLINET Online and OhioLINK improve turnaround times because they eliminate a large chunk of the work associated with processing ILL requests, and workloads are partially shifted to other units of the library. Given the inability of interlibrary loan staff to meet current levels of demand, it is almost certain that libraries using these new systems will begin to experience capacity problems unless resources are allocated to handle the increased levels of activity that these new systems stimulate.

The certainty that capacity problems will arise is rooted in simple economics. As the level of service increases, more users will take advantage of that service, the growth will continue until all demands for the service are saturated. In for-profit organizations, one can use price to influence demand and supply, but in service-oriented, nonprofit organizations such as libraries, there is no easy way to keep demand and supply in equilibrium. There are no painless policies that prevent demand for a popular service from exceeding the system's capacity to supply the service. In a library setting, a popular service may continue to grow until the staff become so overloaded they cannot meet users' demands in a timely manner. When this point is reached, the timeliness and quality of service drops. Eventually, user demand plateaus or can actually decline if users become dissatisfied. If such a condition occurs with statewide and multitype networks such as OhioLINK and ILLINET, they could eventually be faced with the same plight that currently afflicts traditional ILL departments today—high costs and capacity problems resulting in staff and user dissatisfaction.

Managing System Growth
To ensure that the next generation of users continue to receive high-quality service, libraries will have to do a better job of managing the growth of new resource-sharing systems. As mentioned previously, currently almost no limitations are placed on users of interlibrary/circulation-type services, and even when fees are charged, they are often absorbed by a library so that the user is not directly affected. There is little incentive for a user to choose wisely before submitting borrowing requests. As demands for service rise, which seems very likely, library managers are going to face tough decisions on how to finance multilibrary interlibrary–circulation systems. To maintain or improve

the quality of their service to users, libraries will have to increase their investments in such resource-sharing systems and/or introduce policies that will keep service demands within manageable bounds. The next sections discuss two such options: fees and rationing.

Fees

The imposition of fees for interlibrary services would engender greater user accountability for the requests that they make. Although a fee might not be pegged to recover all costs of the service, it could be established at a level that would cause users to evaluate their requests before submitting them, but not so high as to deter them from utilizing the service. For example, "Is this article worth two dollars to me?" Instead of requesting ten items, a user may reevaluate the list and select the five that are the most needed.

Managers should proceed with caution when deciding whether to institute user fees for interlibrary services. In a study conducted by Mark T. Kinnucan, faculty members and graduate students at Ohio universities were interviewed regarding the likelihood of using ILL services or commercial delivery services in hypothetical cases.[24] One part of the survey asked the participants if they were likely to use ILL services if fees were imposed. The survey found that the likelihood of ILL use decreased significantly as the amount of the fee increased. Faculty and students indicated a 94 percent chance of their using ILL if the service were free, a 52 percent chance if the service cost $6, and only a 42 percent chance if the service cost $9. Kinnucan concluded that cost was the issue about which the participants were most sensitive when deciding whether to use ILL or commercial delivery services.[25]

Another study on the effects of cost on ILL, conducted by James H. Sweetland and Darlene E. Weingand at the State Historical Society of Wisconsin, found that the imposition of a $5 fee for ILL services did not result in a significant decline in academic library use of the society's ILL services but did result in a decline in public libraries' use of the collections.[26] The authors admit that their statistics may reflect the tendency of academic libraries to absorb the fee whereas, public libraries are more likely to pass the fee on to the user. Sweetland and Weingand then remark that the imposition of the fee may have encouraged users at public libraries to focus their requests so that an original desire for six microfilm reels becomes a request for only one reel.[27] Because libraries are service organizations and because it seems clear that the imposition of fees will deter some potential users, librarians will have to carefully weigh the possible benefits of staff and procedural efficiencies against the impact of fees on service equity.

Rationing

Another way to mange growth is to impose a limitation on the number of requests each user could make during a predetermined period of time. For example, the library might stipulate that each user is allowed only five requests per year, and at the sixth request a charge would be assessed. Such a policy would indicate more clearly to the user that the library wants to make certain that users make responsible, thoughtful demands of the system and make clear that staff simply are unable to fill infinite demands. But like the imposition of fees, rationing policies should be weighed carefully before their implementation to avoid sending out the mixed messages promising a network with extensive access but limiting access with restrictive policies.

Transformational Model

In addition to fees and rationing, another much more user-oriented option is worthy of consideration. To help users make more informed choices, reduce the possibility of superfluous requests, and at the same time improve the quality of services, why not create an exciting new vision of service that totally transforms traditional assumptions about information and document access services?

Again, Sean is the representative user. Today, he has brought two student colleagues and their physics professor, Arthur Rich, to the library. They are searching for information about the abandonment of the superconducting supercollider project in 1993. The professor is part of a team that will soon testify before a congressional committee considering resurrection of the project. It is commonly believed that the supercollider project was canceled because of political reactions to massive cost overruns, but the scientific community is also aware that a variety of design problems plagued the project. The group entering the library is on a mission to ascertain what those problems actually were. The information will be used to prepare for the congressional testimony. Because several years have passed since the supercollider project was shut down, quite a bit of information has become available.

When Sean and his colleagues enter the library, they find that a lot of changes have occurred since their last visit. Instead of going to the ILL office that was formerly hidden in a distant corner of the main floor, the group spies a large service area that clearly tells them that "if they are looking for information," this is the place to go. The group is welcomed by a librarian (her position as an information specialist is clearly identified) who asks how she can help them. Sean begins the interview and then asks Professor Rich to take over. He explains their mission, and the librarian initiates a series of searches using tools such as bibliographic and full-text databases. She identifies a variety of documents, reports, journal articles, and monographs as possible sources. The documents are in a variety of formats including a full-text digitized format.

The librarian checks the local OPAC, which includes bibliographic and holdings information for all monographs and serials. (The library recently began to include article-level information for the most popular journals, but this information is incomplete.) This search reveals that the library presently owns about half the titles identified in the searches. The rest will have to be obtained from other sources. The librarian checks with the group to gain a better understanding of their deadline. For example, are all of them needed at the same time? She learns that the group is willing to set priorities, and she is able to inform them that the library can request some of the documents from regional libraries but that a few days will be required before delivery can be expected and the transactions will not involve any fees. The library will order other items from commercial document delivery firms and fees will be assessed. One document will be requested from a West Coast library, and if that library is not able to supply it, other sources will be tried. It might take several weeks to acquire this document. The group informs the librarian that up to three weeks would be acceptable, but no longer.

The group leaves the library with a strong sense that they had been helped. Reflecting on his recent experience with ILL, Sean is impressed with the quality and thoroughness of this new service. Instead of leaving the library with feelings of uncertaintyhe has a real sense of what to expect and when.[28]

Redesigned information and document access services could revolutionize traditional interlibrary services. First of all, users would not only understand more about the interlibrary services available and be able to make decisions more appropriate to their needs, they would also see that their requests were entered and the process of locating the items initiated. The personal and tailored service provided through the interview would help to assure users that the library is aware of their specific needs and is working to meet them. The request would no longer appear subject to the fates, but determined by the library and the user together.

The new service paradigm would not cut costs; to the contrary, it would undoubtedly require significant additional funding. For such a vision to become a reality, the library will have to rethink and reconfigure its public services budget. If such a transformation took place, one could make a strong case that a user-oriented service paradigm shift had taken place.

What's the Future of Interlibrary Loan?

The authors cannot end this examination of interlibrary loan/circulation services from a user's perspective without at least acknowledging the impact of the developments they envision on existing interlibrary units and their staff. These developments include systems that enable users to obtain materials from distant locations without having to work through ILL operations (e.g., systems such as OhioLINK). Will such developments signal the end of ILL units? It seems perfectly plausible to expect officials, who are always on the prowl for dollar savings, to begin questioning the need to continue traditional ILL services as new service models emerge. An ILL librarian could easily view such prospects as a threat to existing jobs, but is that necessarily the case?

Instead of representing a threat, these developments could actually prove to be a boon to ILL operations. Instead of devoting the bulk of staff resources to handling requests for materials that users can easily find on databases such as OCLC, the staff could focus their energies and expertise on locating and obtaining materials that users are least likely to locate working on their own, such as dissertations, grey literature, patents, conference proceedings, etc. At present, it is often difficult for staff to pursue fugitive items because of day-to-day pressures to maximize productivity by concentrating on easy-to-find items. The pursuit of fugitive material by ILL would result in a significant value-added service that frequently is unavailable today. Such expertise would fit nicely into the exciting one-stop shopping service models.

Conclusion

Some might argue that personalized, in-house services are theoretically at odds with an electronic network that allows for remote access, with browsing that leaps beyond library walls and state borders and with user autonomy in decision-making. Theoretically, those who would make such an argument would be correct. However, in developing systems that increase access capabilities beyond anyone's wildest dreams, libraries are likely to create a situation similar to that which occurred in the 1970s when they had to admit (privately, if not publicly) that they were simply unable to supply users with absolutely everything, either by acquisition or resource-sharing. By the natural laws of physics, every system has its limits, and libraries may benefit in the long run from anticipating early on those boundaries at the end of the road and implementing procedures that enable library staff to provide the best service possible despite those limitations.

Whatever service models are employed in the era of networks and digital libraries, the fundamental factors in the equation will still remain: tight budgets, the eternal wish for more staff, and the needs of users, many of whom will continue to require the help of bibliographical sleuths. Even major systems such as ILLINET Online and OhioLINK, which appear to streamline procedures and to allow user autonomy in a way never before possible, are still faced with serious monetary concerns. And in considering the needs of the user, it is important to keep in mind that not every user is alike, or like our friend, Sean. Some users have a multitude of items they wish to request through interlibrary loan, some users want six articles faxed to them by the end of the day, some users want a rare folio from Italy, and others do not even know that interlibrary loan exists or what it means.

In the best-case scenario, Sean would like to obtain the needed article well before the paper's due date, in a legible reproduction of the original, with relatively little hassle and at no charge. Perhaps a library may not be able to fulfill all of Sean's dreams; if not, librarians need to prioritize their service and develop an interlibrary system that meets as many of these objectives as possible. Whether personalized attention combined with efficiency can be achieved best through face-to-face interaction or through an electronic network that presents a variety of choices to the user is as yet unknown.

Librarians must decide which kind of model works best with their institution and the needs of their specific users. Although the limitations of the institution's staff and equipment should be considered in the decision-making process, librarians need to find the best way to provide high-quality service to their users, in both offering access to information and helping to locate the information sought. Ultimately, the best combination interlibrary–circulation system is the one that tries to meet the needs of each user in the most efficient manner possible.

Notes

1. Hugh C. Atkinson, "Resource Sharing," in *Collection Management in Public Libraries* (Chicago: ALA, 1986), 39.

2. Sean's saga is based on a composite of ILL interactions and is not based on experiences with a single library's ILL service.

3. Shirley K. Baker and Mary E. Jackson, *Maximizing Access, Minimizing Cost: A First Step toward the Information Access Future* (Washington, D.C.: Association of Research Libraries, Nov. 1992, rev. Feb. 1993), 3.

4. Mary E. Jackson, "Library to Library: Fitting the Bill," *Wilson Library Bulletin* 66 (June 1992): 97.

5. Baker and Jackson, *Maximizing Access, Minimizing Cost*, 3.

6. Sarah Pritchard, "ARL Statistics Show Shift from Ownership to Access," *ARL* 161 (Mar. 2, 1992), 3.

7. Suzanne D. Gyeszly and Gary O. Allen, "Effects of Online Periodical Indexes on Interlibrary Loan Services and Collection Development," *Journal of Interlibrary Loan and Information Supply* 1, no.3 (1991): 48.

8. Processing ILL requests is a far more complicated process than the uninitiated may realize, but procedures are not the focus of this paper. For a more detailed description of procedures, see Lois C. Gilmer, *Interlibrary Loan: Theory and Management* (Englewood, Colo.: Libraries Unlimited, 1994), 264.

9. See section 5.5 of the National Interlibrary Loan Code for the United States, 1993, *RQ* 33:4 (summer 1994): 479.

10. See generally, Rosanna M. O'Neil, *Total Quality Management in Libraries: A Sourcebook,* (Englewood, Colo.: Libraries Unlimited, Inc., 1994).

11. Tom Whitehall, "Quality in Library and Information Service: A Review," *Total Quality Management in Libraries: A Sourcebook* (Englewood, Colo.: Libraries Unlimited, Inc., 1994), 110.

12. Baker and Jackson, *Maximizing Access, Minimizing Cost,* 9.

13. Amy Chang, "Computerizing Communication for Interlibrary Loan," *College & Research Libraries News* 50 (Dec. 1989): 992–94.

14. Ibid., 993.

15. See Michael S. Barnett, Rodney C. Bruce, Dale K. Carrison, et al., "MSUS/PALS: Building a Regional Information Infrastructure," *Library Hi Tech* 12 no. 1 (1994): 7–34.

16. Ibid., 20, 22.

17. Shari Chapman and Mary Kay Smith, "Sidebar 4: How PALS Interlibrary Loan Impacts an Interlibrary Loan Department," *Library Hi Tech* 12, no. 1 (1994): 23–24.

18. The CIC's virtual electronic library (VEL) now under development is another example of an innovative one-stop service model. For more information on VEL, see Barbara McFadden Allen, "The CIC Virtual Electronic Library Integrates Resources and Services," *OCLC Newsletter,* Nov./Dec. 1997, 28.

19. See Bernard G. Sloan, "ILLINET Online: Resource Sharing in Illinois," *Advances in Library Resource Sharing* 2 (1992) 100–107; ———, "Resource Sharing in Times of Retrenchment," *Library Administration and Management* 6, no. 1 (1992): 26–28.

20. ———, *Linked Systems for Resource Sharing* (Boston: G.K. Hall & Co., 1991), 8.

21. Sloan, "Resource Sharing in Times of Retrenchment," 27.

22. Scott Van Dam, Jennifer Block, and Richard N. Pettit Jr., "The Impact of the OhioLINK Network on Traditional Interlibrary Loan," *Journal of Interlibrary Loan, Document Delivery and Information Supply* 8, no 1 (1997): 1–19.

23. David F. Kohl, "OhioLINK: Plugging into Progress," *Library Journal* 118 (Oct, 1, 1993): 44.

24. Mark T. Kinnucan, "Demand for Document Delivery and Interlibrary Loan in Academic Settings," *Library & Information Science Research* 15 (fall 1993): 368.

25. Ibid., 372.

26. James H. Sweetland and Darlene E. Weingand, "Interlibrary Loan Transaction Fees in a Major Research Library: They Don't Stop the Borrowers," *Library & Information Research* 12 (Jan.1990): 96–97.

27. Ibid., 98.

28. What happened in the library? It had recently reorganized itself so that patrons (customers) now enjoy one-stop shopping when they seek information and documents. The library's document delivery units were consolidated to provide the utmost in customer responsiveness and operational efficiency.

Value-Added Access Services

Lynn Wiley and John Harer

The circulation function of the library is so fundamental to library activity that one could define libraries in terms of circulation: for example; an institution that owns one book and allows people to use it is a library, and an institution that may have a million books and does not allow anyone to use them may simply be a museum.[1]

Right after library science school, one of the authors accepted a professional position in a small library at a major research institution. She was well acquainted with those who used the library and could serve them personally with the resources they required. The library's patrons did not need to, indeed most could not, go to the closed stacks; decipher the idiosyncratic ways of the card catalog with its unique classification and filing system; initiate an interlibrary loan request; or even copy articles on the one poor machine available. The librarian did bibliographic searching, retrieving, copying, interlibrary loaning, recalling, and claiming. It was a very satisfying and rewarding first job. However, as the author looks back on that experience, she wonders about the frustrated patrons, who just wanted to get what they needed, when they needed it, without assistance. Were there patrons who became disgusted with the archaic access and with policy restrictions in obtaining the physical material and simply gave up in frustration? Librarians argue that they want self-sufficient and independent users, but they do not always make that possible.

The authors' experience in circulation work has enabled them to identify and break down barriers to excellent customer service. Those barriers are not usually intentional but generally are a product of history, growth, and organizational structure. Understanding the origins of an organizational structure or a service policy can provide the basis for productive and adaptive change. This chapter looks specifically at the history, role, and functions of circulation services, the special relationship circulation has with the library user, and the services now available that give clients new options in using the library.

Circulation and Customer Services

Circulation services (loan desk, access services, by any name, the activities that deliver the physical information to the patron) have more contact with users than any other. Users often form their impressions of libraries from the outcomes of those interactions. Putting people first must be circulation's primary objective. Customer service literature shows that:

> Many customers do not complain before they leave, they just leave. But, they frequently tell their friends about their bad experiences. Studies have shown that a dissatisfied customer on average tells twice as many people as a satisfied customer. . . . The bottom line is that all of the major causes of customer dissatisfaction are strongly linked to human performance. Therefore an organization's staff has the greatest impact on the satisfaction of its customers.[2]

Academic library patrons are clients and, yes, customers. Libraries provide a product that enhances their access to information. Patrons, as customers, have expectations and buy information at the cost of their own time and convenience. Libraries want and need clients that come back. Libraries face competition from fee-based information services, the World Wide Web, and other computer-based resources. In order to maintain the academic library as a vital component of higher education, libraries need to provide a value-added service.

Even though they work diligently to identify, interpret, and deliver their patrons' information needs, librarians do not often put themselves in their patrons' shoes to see the barriers that have been erected. Small college libraries and academic departmental libraries may still provide a highly personalized service, but for most academic institutions, small libraries are no longer feasible. Libraries have become increasingly complex. The numbers of staff, especially professional staff, have declined despite the increasing volume of work. In many cases, professionals are removed from the front line. In attempting to carry out day-to-day operations, librarians have evolved policies and organizational structures to get essential work done in ways that do not always have the user in mind. Sheila S. Intner put it well:

> Why should the library client always be wrong? Why should lay people have to think like librarians to use libraries? We can adopt an approach that has proved its worth in business and begin with the assumption that the customer (i.e., the library user) is always right. Instead of looking at things the way a librarian does, we can look at them the way the customer does.[3]

Stephen K. Stoan goes further in summarizing faculty use of libraries:

> Faculty complaints . . . derive in no small measure from the (faculty) perception that, not understanding research, librarians end up organizing the library, its services, and its resources in terms of their own logic, not that of researchers.[4]

This chapter addresses the barriers to people-oriented circulation service and discusses the value systems that need to be changed before such service can be implemented.

Circulation Services: A Brief History

Academic libraries have not always been about people. Over 60 years ago, Charles Harvey Brown and H. G. Bousfield, in their classic book on circulation work, described how libraries had perceived their role:

College and University libraries are old in years; but from the standpoint of use they are very young. Formerly they were storehouses rather than laboratories and even now in some institutions, practices more fitting for storehouses than for laboratories are found in operation.[5]

As storehouses, libraries closed their stacks and in some cases allowed no access to undergraduates. Books were for upperclassmen or faculty only.

Brown and Bousfield called for a clean break from this past and identified the important role that circulation services plays in satisfying users. They recognized that the circulation or loan librarian was a critical link between the users and library resources:

The first contact which students make with a college library (in many cases with any library) is through the loan department. The only contact ever made by many students with a large collection of books is through assistance of the loan department of their college library. Loan desk practices will in many cases determine whether students continue the use of books throughout their college course, or whether they become discouraged at failures to obtain desired material promptly.[6]

They argued that the "loan department should be something more than a passive agency." The department should not only supply books, but also "stimulate, expand, and increase the intellectual needs of its readers."[7] Brown and Bousfield were visionaries, but their views were dismissed in favor of business practices. As Deborah A. Carver noted in her excellent article on the development of access services, Brown and Bousfield's views were not widely adopted for circulation operations. In fact, the trend in libraries was to reduce the professional contact because circulation work was seen as more production than people oriented. Libraries, at mid-century, were forced to cope with increasing student populations and growing acquisitions budgets. Acquisitions budgets were growing not only because of larger student bodies, but also because of expansive collection development policies. New, roomier buildings were constructed to hold these larger collections. Controlling access to the collection became more mechanized to cope with a higher volume of activity. Carver points out: "By the end of World War II, a stripped down mechanized, clerically-staffed circulation department replaced the broader concept so fondly documented by Brown and Bousefield."[8] Libraries, borrowing practices from industry, broke down duties into discrete responsibilities and stressed efficiency. Carver shows that such specialization led to increased hierarchy within units and departments with a resulting fragmentation of larger goals as each unit competed for the same resources to complete its work. Library users theoretically had access to much more information, if they could figure out how to get it. As Richard M. Dougherty relates: "Collections become more difficult to use as they grow larger and more decentralized. . . . The size and richness of a library collection must be balanced with its complexity and accessibility."[9] In achieving the goal of building larger collections, libraries were thwarted in their ability to serve users effectively.

Library staff, as well as library users, are affected by the hierarchical nature of library work. According to one observer:

> In conducting in house training sessions for staff of large library systems, the staff members sometimes do not really know each other or understand what other departmental staff do, although they frequently offer related services and should consider themselves part of a team. Instead they view themselves as rivals for limited dollars or limited customers.[10]

The Business of Circulation
Services to Users
As previously noted, circulation staff have the highest number of public interactions with patrons. Because users may ask any staff member any question, circulation staff also must be able to provide answers to myriad questions about the library. The front line in a triage system, they are frequently asked how to identify materials, how to find the materials identified, and what to do when the materials cannot be located. Patrons may be unfamiliar with libraries, may make mistakes in

searching catalogs, or may fail to find an item even though it is in its proper place. Items may be charged or lost. To be able to confidently help users in each of these situations, staff must be given a thorough orientation to the library, the services, the building layout, and the basic tenet that they are there to help the patron. As the library's front line, circulation staff can alert the appropriate agencies to deficiencies in signage and training. Although answering inquiries is a significant part of circulation service, it is largely unrecognized. Staff need training in answering queries. For example, they need instruction on how to conduct an interview to comprehend the question. They also need to understand when to answer a question and when to refer it to a librarian. Reference personnel can help train circulation staff to answer questions. Involving reference staff in circulation training has the added benefit of making circulation personnel more informed about the reference department's staff and services.

In addition to answering questions, circulation staff are frequently called upon to interpret and enforce library policies. Circulation services is one area of library service where a body of policies is consistently formulated and implemented. Everyone has had the experience of being told at a customer service desk, "Sorry that's the policy here . . .," end of discussion. Flexibility combined with an articulate rationale behind a body of policies are steps to better relations and better service.

Where do policies come from, and whom do they serve? Although policies are very necessary because they govern when, how, where materials may be used, and by whom, they are often developed in reaction to problems rather than carefully drawn to address service needs.[11] Often policies do not include reviews or evaluations to see if they are achieving their goals. Libraries tend to set polices but then fail to judge their efficacy or modify the ones that are not successful until outside forces prompt a change.

"They are adopted at one stage in a library's development in response to certain conditions and then preserved . . . they are maintained even though no one can quite remember why such rules were established; even though no one can explain the rationale behind them to a patron with a question about a particular policy; and despite staffing, workflow and technological changes which existing policies do not address or cannot accommodate."[12]

A comparison of circulation policies at peer institutions is sometimes used to review policies at one's own institution. Merri A. Hartse and Daniel R. Lee used this method to support changes in their institution's circulation policies.[13] Although peer comparisons can be very helpful to point out trends and omissions, or to garner support for changes, policies must serve the needs of the institution's users.

Policies must have a framework. The best policies balance users' needs against library resources. Policies should ensure fair treatment and not create barriers to service. At the same time, to achieve fair access to materials and services for all users, some users may occasionally be inconvenienced. Academic libraries should arm themselves with better understanding of user needs and build a program to reasonably address these needs. This program should provide a balance between expectations and known limitations, and should offer choices to clients.

To develop a coherent program tied to user needs, libraries need information, but as one recent article states:

> libraries have made it their stock-in-trade to keep use
> statistics and to undertake use studies. It is less common to
> see extensive user studies, especially among academic
> libraries.[14]

However, some libraries, borrowing the techniques from business marketing, are using focus groups to obtain feedback from the user's perspective. Focus group studies may be expensive, but the expense does not exceed the risks of implementing a service program that does not meet common needs.[15]

The loan policies of a library will dictate how long items may circulate, to whom, and if they can be renewed. In pioneering research, Michael K. Buckland investigated the effect of loan periods on book availability. Buckland found that:

- For any given loan period, the chances of a copy being on
  the shelves when sought varies inversely with the
  popularity of the book.

- For any loan period, the length of the loan period and the immediate availability are inversely related.
- For a given level of immediate availability, the popularity and the length of the loan period are necessarily also related. The greater the popularity, the shorter the loan period has to be: the less the popularity, the longer the loan period can be.
- Increasing the number of copies available, like shortening the loan period, increases immediate availability.[16]

He concluded that librarians may provide adaptive controls by continually watching loan periods and offering variable loans for higher-use items.

Buckland's study was done before the widespread use of integrated library systems. Patrons in most libraries may now determine if an item is charged out to another user and may even be able to initiate a recall or place a hold online. Many library consortia provide access to "metacollections," or union catalogs of their holdings where patrons may "request" delivery of loans as needed. Document delivery can offer fast solutions for unavailable items, whether not on the shelf or never acquired. Interlibrary loan has expedited fulfillment of requests with courier delivery services. These options may have made the length of loan periods less important. Nevertheless, libraries should be aware of the effect of loan periods on availability and conduct their own research using statistical packages now available with automated circulation systems to analyze the impacts of their loan policies.

Policies about fines and fining require special attention. Users perceive circulation not as a facilitator of information access but more the enforcer of rules. Fining and billing policies and subsequent suspensions of borrowing privileges drive that image. Yet, it is surprising how little is understood about the effectiveness of fines. "Many librarians have expressed dissatisfaction with the use of fines and other sanctions."[17] Librarians have learned what psychologists have long recognized: negative reinforcement may be necessary but may also bring many undesirable side effects. Sheila S. Intner, summarizing a comparison of library policies, notes that:

> Very few librarians expressed a desire to raise fines . . . even
> in those libraries where fines had been raised in the recent
> past, there seemed to be a lack of confidence that this alone
> was effective in deterring non-returns.[18]

Fines may not work but are maintained because no alternative has been found. Are there alternatives? W. Bede Mitchell suggests a more positive approach to minimizing overdues. He suggests rewarding patrons for returning items on time rather than penalize them for overdues.[19] Some libraries may decide to assess fines only for serious offenses, no response to recalls, for example, to make them more effective. Selective fining may prevent users from dismissing yet another library notice in their mailbox by consigning it to the trash unread.

Another approach is to look at what fines are supposed to do and to try to make them more effective. The reason for fines is to encourage return. Can libraries remove some of the negative connotation of fines by calling them long term rental fees, fees like those at video stores? These long-term rental fees would be invoked only after significant delay and warnings issued in the form of notices. Libraries that have adopted one fee for late returns have done so largely because it is so costly to maintain the nickel-and-dime approach of daily fines. One simple fee, assessed at a consistent time after the item is due, say 30 days, is easy to implement and communicate. The policy may easily be reinforced with signs, notices, statements on overdues, and by asking first-time users to sign a formal document notifying them that they have entered into an agreement with the library. Policies and penalties would be detailed along with ways to avoid said penalties. Giving patrons direct access to circulation records, or explaining how they can access them if direct access is not possible, will also make these fees more palatable. A liberal renewal policy coupled with a very strict recall policy is recommended. Users should be able to renew in person, by phone, or on some automated circulation system by self-renewal. Circulation staff should consider adding book drops and expanding hours to make it easier for users to return materials.

When fines or fees are unavoidable, payment should be easy. Bill payment options should be extensive. Clemency programs should be available and consistent. A separate billing desk staffed with courteous and well-trained employees is very helpful in clearing up problems and restoring goodwill.

Finally, there is the question of faculty overdues. Even though libraries are democratic institutions and the preferential treatment of faculty seems undemocratic, faculty often receive longer loan periods, automatic renewals, and no fines. It is important to understand, however, that faculty will be using the library facilities longer than any other group. They can be libraries' strongest support, because they rely on libraries for their own research and teaching. Libraries should foster this symbiotic relationship and work to remove possible conflicts. A policy of preferred renewal treatment with an outside limitation and an agreement for adherence to a universal recall program may be effective. If this results in additional costs because it is necessary to buy more duplicates or to monitor faculty charges, the gain in public relations is worth it.

As important as it is to have well-developed, user-centered policies and procedures, it is equally important that all members of the staff have full knowledge of these policies and flexibility when applying them. Not all rules can or should be rigidly enforced. Some noncirculating material can be photocopied; some weekend users can be given temporary permits, although the office is closed; and disabled users can be given services denied others. Many staff members in hierarchical organizations are fearful of making exceptions. Johanna Rediger Bradley observed circulation operations at an urban university. She found that even though staff members thought they knew circulation policies, there was a disparity in the way they enforced them. Some staff members routinely denied service even when the policies allowed for some discretion. Some users, unwilling to be thwarted, either became belligerent or took their complaint to a higher authority, occasionally the library director. The original decision was often overruled but not without unpleasantness. Bradley found that the reference staff, even those members who were not professional, handled customer relations better.[20]

Collection Maintenance

The core of circulation work is the availability of material. The effect of loan periods on availability was discussed earlier in this chapter, but library materials are sometimes not available for other reasons. Problems in access may be due to library errors, such as mistakes in shelving, labeling, or cataloging. The material may be returned but not re-shelved or may be at the bindery. The availability of materials is dependent on good stack maintenance. Whether stacks are closed or open, the volumes must be shelved correctly and in a timely manner. Open stacks provide direct access to the user and permit browsing but need more maintenance. Closed stacks necessitate retrieval on demand, which is labor-intensive and requires well-trained staff. In either case, absolute priority must be given to supporting the work needed to maintain orderly, accessible material. Staff must be available to re-shelve both returns and materials used in-house, read and order the shelves, and shift collections as needed. All the work that goes into selecting, acquiring, processing, cataloging, and housing an item is wasted if it cannot be found when needed. All of this may seem obvious, but it is vital and shows that new attitudes must be accompanied by old essentials.

Stack maintenance should also include binding and preservation. Circulation staff not only see more users, they also see the most heavily used items, those that must be referred for special care, such as rebinding or other preservation treatments. They routinely identify items with missing pages and those with covers on their last legs. Skilled staff can save a volume before it becomes an unusable catastrophe. Circulation staff should have the best training in procedures for proper book handling, the correct way to remove a book from the shelf and how to photocopy it. Well-trained staff can mentor and train new student workers.

Managing the book stacks is a complex responsibility. Technology has offered some new opportunities to analyze and refine services and increase access. Circulation is responsible for managing access to individual items. *Inventory* or *stock control* are terms often used, not just for stack maintenance, but also for other activities that ensure the availability of items. In many integrated systems, the public can see whether an item is on the shelf, checked out, or in a special location. Because the accuracy of these records affects access, circulation must oversee these records and report or fix mistakes in status or links between the catalog record and the holdings statement. Most of these errors will be identified at the checkout point, when a user is charging out material or paging it, from either closed stacks or a remote storage facility. A wrong record may appear, an item may not be linked to an actual record, the copy or holding information may be incorrect or incomplete, the location may be wrong, the piece may be improperly coded as noncirculating, or the spine label may be incorrect. Circulation staff, when properly trained, can correct many of these problems, linking the record to the piece or even creating a brief circulation record so that an item can circulate, eliminating patron delays while maximizing stock control. Although most libraries cannot undertake a large-scale inventory project, it is possible to maintain control at the point of use. Inventories of high-use areas are also feasible now because portable bar-code readers allow staff to "read" the shelves, resolve status problems, identify missing titles, and record inaccuracies. Although it is not always possible to catch the previously described errors, well trained staff stand a better chance, and library clientele appreciate staff that can efficiently solve problems.

Circulation collects data on lost or billed books, items with multiple recalls, search results on missing items, and information on high-use titles. These are all valuable for collection development. Staff in acquisitions or collection development need to know when to reorder lost or missing books and when to order additional copies of a title. If the circulation or access department is responsible for interlibrary borrowing, loan requests can indicate any gaps in the collection. Options in document delivery now make possible buying on demand in selected areas rather then comprehensively collecting. Interlibrary borrowing data on use, costs, and turnaround can help make decisions on purchases. Circulation also collects data on who uses what and when, which can be invaluable information for collection policy assessment.

Resource security is another basic concern for the circulation department. The fears of the librarians of the nineteenth century are being realized in today's libraries. Theft and vandalism reduce the value of the collection as an asset, but more important, limit the access to information for the library's clientele. When libraries were much smaller, collections came under a more watchful eye. Patrons would be hard-pressed to tear pages out of material because the library staff were usually in close proximity. The minimum standard for security should be some control of the exits of the building. Although an electronic security system is a viable response for many libraries, it is a mechanical form of deterrence that is not foolproof. Fair and effective performance in security procedures should take into account the following phenomena:

- Not all thefts are intentional: forgetfulness and haste are common, human errors. Policies for handling those activating a book security system should take such factors into account.[21]
- Not all "thefts" represent a permanent loss: many items are simply illegally borrowed and are returned as if they were checked out.
- Not all "thefts" are by library patrons: employee theft is not confined to the private sector. Security policies and systems should address employee theft.
- Not all losses are due to thefts: mutilation is still a problem which may result from, at least in part, inadequate photocopy facilities and ineffective book security systems.[22]

Auxiliary Services

Circulation, as a part of their service operations, traditionally provides and manages a host of auxiliary services designed to enhance user access. Although these services are often seen as secondary, they are of primary importance to the patron. Basic patron needs include: safe, clean, well-lit, comfortable study areas, and well-maintained copiers that are operated at a reasonable price with options that eliminate the need for change.

The circulation unit typically is the one that handles building security issues because it opens and closes the building daily. If building use is restricted, circulation staff may guard the doors to limit access to appropriate patrons. Fire drills and any emergency building evacuation are generally within the province of circulation. Staff should be well trained in emergency procedures.

Circulation often assigns and manages study spaces or carrels. These services make it possible for patrons to use the material on-site.

Large noncirculating collections, in particular, mandate provision for in-house use. Expanding the number of seats available, providing access to food and drink, issuing universal copy cards, creating drop-off copy centers, are services to consider. An argument can also be made for the provision of a place where users can purchase pens, paper, and diskettes to be sure that they can make full use of the collection. Vending machines may be the answer, both because many needs can be met by the products that may be offered for sale this way and because good partnerships with vendors may result in other benefits. Many times, contracts with copy service providers will include support for change machines.

Circulation usually monitors and often maintains copying machines. In some libraries, it is responsible for the management of an on-site copy center. The selection of photocopiers is an important decision. Ideally, libraries want the perpetual-motion machine of copiers, one that never breaks down, but also replenishes its own supplies. Of course, no such machine exists, but copier technology that is minimally disruptive to other library operations already exists. Having enough copiers to meet the needs of the users is paramount, and having reliable, working copiers is necessary to establish a realistic photocopy service. In addition, staff must be trained to deal with mechanical breakdowns, including paper jams; replenishment of supplies; and instruction of patrons on use of the copier. The library's goal should be the acquisition of self-service copiers that have proved to be low in mechanical breakdowns and paper jams, have the highest-supply capacity, and are intuitively easy to use. Good facilities for copying deter vandalism to the collections.

Technology

Integrated online systems have revolutionized circulation, eliminating much labor-intensive work. Charging, discharging, and other aspects of inventory control are faster and easier. Recall and overdue notices and bills are more efficient, timely, and accurate. Circulation staff have a greater opportunity to interact with the patrons.

Self-service has exploded across the marketplace. The American love of independence drives the continual expansion of self-service. Banks, gas stations, grocery stores, pharmacies, and mail-order stores have successfully exploited the self-service mentality to reduce costs and increase customer satisfaction. Libraries are also realizing the possibilities. Self-checkout systems allow patrons to check out their own material. Besides convenience and control, patron confidentiality is increased. Some online vendors also provide access to self-service options such as renewals, recalls, holds, requests of books from other libraries, and access to individual records.

Nancy Larsen Helmick has described how The Ohio State University saved resources and enhanced service with use of innovative technology. Renewals and recalls were made self-service because the library unit responsible could not keep up with demand. Self-service was overwhelmingly successful from the patron's point of view, and it did succeed in freeing up staff. Helmick remarks that: "Library staff will be encouraged to try more adventuresome experimentation once they realize that the number of patrons served increase even as staff and equipment resources level off and the number of routine activities at staff-assisted stations decreases, allowing expansion of services for more needy patrons."[23]

Jackie Mardikian has written a literature survey about self-charge systems across different sectors. In summarizing Bateson's research regarding consumer reaction to self-service, she reports that:

> a large percentage of customers chose the do it yourself option over the traditional service option. This was the preferred option even when self-serve did not offer the consumer any incentives such as discounts or convenience ... that if an individual is already using a self-serve option in one industry it is highly likely that he or she would use that option in another service scenario. Time and control were listed as the most important dimensions in making choices. Perception of control over the outcome of the transaction seems to be the most important contributing factor in selecting one type of service over another.[24]

The Internet has also opened up tremendous opportunities for the information seeker. Libraries, harnessing the Web, can offer new services that both instruct and inform while taking requests. Many libraries are exploring new service options with Web reference forms, renewal requests, suggestions for book orders, and interlibrary loan requests.

Giving patrons control and choices widens access. It brings libraries closer to a model of the self-sufficient independent user and frees the library staff to work on the library's infrastructure and provide more individual attention to users who have nonroutine matters.

Conclusion

The circulation department offers the best view of library users. Because circulation staff are busy reacting all day to user queries, problems, and demands, they have countless opportunities to provide services to patrons. To provide these services, staff must be trained to answer questions correctly and to know when and how to properly refer users to others. They must also understand library policies, be able to explain them clearly, and apply them with discretion as circumstance dictates. Circulation policies should maximize collection use and maintain the collection. Users are best served when the collections are properly and promptly shelved and when the staff are trained to preserve and maintain them. Technology can free staff from routine tasks, allowing them to offer users with problems greater assistance.

Notes

1. Hugh C. Atkinson, "Circulation Automation," *Advances in Librarianship* 4 (1974): 63.

2. Arlene Farber Sirkin, "Customer Service: Another Side of TQM," *Journal of Library Administration* 18, nos. 1–2 (1993): 79.

3. Sheila S. Intner, *Interfaces: Relationships between Library Technical and Public Services* (Englewood, Colo.: Libraries Unlimited, 1993), 43.

4. Stephen K. Stoan, "Research and Library Skills: An Analysis and Interpretation," *College & Research Libraries* 45 (Mar. 1984): 99.

5. Charles Harvey Brown and H.G. Bousfield, *Circulation Work in College and University Libraries* (Chicago: ALA, 1933), 7.

6. Ibid., 11–12.

7. Ibid., 34.

8. Deborah A. Carver, "From Circulation to Access Services: The Shift in Academic Library Organization," *Collection Management* 17, nos. 1-2 (1992): 27.

9. Richard M. Dougherty, "Needed: User-Responsive Research Libraries," *Library Journal* 116 (Jan. 1991): 59.

10. Sirkin, "Customer Service," 76.

11. Duane Webster, *Library Policies: Analysis, Formulation, and Use in Academic Institutions*, Office of University Library Management Studies. Occasional Papers, no. 2 (Washington, D.C.: Association of Research Libraries, 1972), 11.

12. Merri A. Hartse and Daniel R. Lee, "Changing Circulation Policies at an ARL Library: The Impact of Peer Institution Survey Data on the Process," *Collection Management* 17, nos. 1–2 (1992): 133.

13. Ibid., 134.

14. Margo Crist, Peggy Daub, and Barbara MacAdam, "User Studies: Reality Check and Future Perfect," *Wilson Library Bulletin* (Feb. 1994): 38.

15. Richard Widdows, Tia A. Hensler, and Marlaya H. Wyncott, "The Focus Group Interview: A Method for Assessing Users' Evaluation of Library Service," *College & Research Libraries* 52 (July 1991): 352–59.

16. Michael K. Buckland, *Book Availability and the Library User*, (New York: Pergamon Pr., 1975), 137.

17. W. Bede Mitchell, "On the Use of Positive Reinforcement to Minimize the Problem of Overdue Library Materials," *Journal of Library Administration* 9, no. 3 (1988): 87.

18. Sheila S. Intner and Josephine Riss Fang, *Technical Services in the Medium Sized Library: An Investigation of Current Practices* (Hamden, Conn.: Library Professional Publications, 1991), 47.

19. Mitchell, "On the Use of Positive Reinforcement," 87.

20. Johanna Rediger Bradley, "Bureaucratic and Individual Knowledge and Action in the Public Service Units of an Academic Library" (Ph.D. diss., Univ. of Illinois at Urbana-Champaign, 1991).

21. James H. Richards Jr., "Missing Inaction," *Journal of Academic Librarianship* 5 (Nov. 1979): 266.

22. Elizabeth Gates Kesler, "A Campaign against Mutilation," *Journal of Academic Librarianship* 3 (Mar. 1977): 29.

23. Nancy Larsen Helmick, "Are Patrons Ready for 'Do it Yourself' Services?" *College & Research Libraries* 53 (Jan. 1992): 48.

24. Jackie Mardikian, "Self-Service Charge Systems: Current Technological Applications and Their Implications for the Future Library" *Reference Services Review* 25, no. 4 (1995).

Toward Self-Sufficient Users: Helping Patrons Learn to Use Information Resources Independently

Stephen J. Smith and Dale S. Montanelli

Access Engineering or Access Artistry?
(Ars sine scientia est nihil. : Art without science is nothing.)

Who are our users as we approach the next millennium? Given the split-second changes of the information age, the answer can change from moment to moment. A realistic answer is quite possibly everybody and anybody, at any time. Further, how do we determine what each of these individual users really wants? Answer: we must ask. Impossible! Not at all. We need only to ask each user at any one time and from any one place. This is the interface and integration of human speed with techno speed. This interface exists and will continue to coexist. Finally, how do we define user self-sufficiency? Individual users can only truly answer this question. Library users have a right to be in control of their lives. Adult users should be respected.

Libraries and Technology

Librarians have long excelled at this role in providing access to the resources (independent of format) held by their own institution. Librarians now need to apply these same skills to organizing resources that are available through new electronic technologies. S. Michael Malinconico recognized this when he reported that:

The professional concerns of many librarians have shifted from the custody and development of physical collections to locating information wherever it may be, moving it to wherever it is needed, and adding *value to it*. Librarians are spending increasing amounts of time engaged in *teaching and learning* in order to help users and their institutions make effective use of the ever expanding kaleidoscope of information resources and services.[1]

The library should be viewed as "the place" people can go to make sense of the information overload that now exists. People need to find the information they want, to understand the limitations of what they find within the context in which they find it, and to develop strategies to resolve conflicts among the answers produced.

Within this evolving paradigm, where does education fit? "Education is the overarching library activity. Education and information literacy focus on the user and not on the librarian or the collections. Education and self-sufficiency are driven by user needs and result in a user product, not a library product."[2] Users "should not have to depend on we librarians to use a library or its resources, but only on us to design and maintain the library so the potential of information retrieval remains a constant possibility."[3] Although we should not and effectively cannot define self-sufficiency for each user, it is clear that self-sufficiency can be sharply enhanced through a certain amount of human interactive instruction.

Library Instruction: Past, Present, Future
Historically, library instruction has focused on the undergraduate student and emphasized the development of those bibliographic skills needed to use library resources for completing class assignments. In the "information age," this limited vision of library instruction has changed.

As libraries introduce computerized systems that people use to access and manipulate information, librarians will increasingly assume the roles of consultants and teachers. They will need to be conversant with many different information systems and be prepared to answer questions regarding the operation and use of those systems and how which system should be used to address particular users' needs.[4]

Educating individuals to become self-reliant users of information is one of the most important and challenging responsibilities facing librarians today. Academic librarians have endorsed the instruction of users for more than 100 years. Instruction concerning the organization, retrieval, and use of information has become an integral component of the service function provided by librarians.

Instruction includes various educational services including library orientation, library instruction, bibliographic instruction, and information management education. Some variant names for these services include user education and instruction for information literacy. According to Lizabeth A. Wilson:

> Today, instruction in the use of libraries goes beyond the walls of the library to the broader concept of *knowledge management*. As the amount of information continues to expand, and as radical changes are made in the way in which information is stored, organized, accessed, and used, it has become increasingly apparent that individuals need instruction not only in the use of libraries but also in the general handling and use of information.[5]

Indeed, the organic nature of information systems indicates that a continuous lifelong learning process is a requisite for users in the information age.

Library instruction began to utilize structured approaches to program development in the 1970s. Instruction at this time included orientation to the library, training in the use of the specific library, education on the use of reference tools, and strategies for searching.[6] By the end of the decade, however, there appeared a significant shift from this tool-based instruction toward concept-based instruction.

In the 1980s, the second generation of bibliographic instructors expanded their base of knowledge. In 1981, the Bibliographic Instruction Section of the Association of College and Research

Libraries sponsored a bibliographic instruction think tank to discuss current ideas and recommend future directions. The result of the think tank was the development of a set of principles that integrated new ideas concerning learning theory, concept-based instruction, critical thinking skills, and new technologies into the structured programs.[7]

> Learning theory generally can be divided into two broad traditions: the behavioral theories and the cognitive theories. Behavioral theories originated in the early part of this century. They assume that knowledge can be broken into smaller units and that knowledge can be measured by changes in behavior. Behavioral theories also assume that the learner is a blank slate or an empty vessel into which knowledge can be poured. These approaches view knowledge as independent of thinking abilities and knowledge acquisition as an additive process. Cognitive theories originated in the late 1970's and 1980's (and) assume that the learner actively interacts with the environment and that each learner creates knowledge which is unique. In this alternative view, knowledge is perceived as a holistic process, not as an additive process, and can only be learned by going back and forth between parts and wholes. Behavioral approaches are centered around the teacher and what the teacher teaches. Cognitive approaches are student-oriented and view the teacher as coach, modeler, or facilitator.[8]

This emphasis on the learner as an active participant in a process more fittingly takes into account the adult learner as an individual. A recognition of the importance of individual difference is particularly important not only because of new technologies, but also because of the growing enrollments of older returning students, minorities, and international students. This diverse pool brings divergent library experiences that necessitate flexible and creative approaches to instruction.

When we design programs to help patrons learn to use information resources independently, we may need to organize this training in ways that are different from those usually taught in educational methods courses. Most of these courses focus on the learner as young and inexperienced, and make assumptions about the learner's motivation that may not be appropriate to the adult library patron. In the academic library, all patrons should be assumed to be adult learners and the training programs designed with the guidance of what is now known about adult learners. By creating instruction programs that are based on cognitive theory, we can help users develop a set of information-finding skills that are transferable to any information system. When we also teach critical thinking skills, users will know how to continuously learn and will be able to thrive in this information age. We should customize such instruction to respect individual learners and their information needs at any given time. Our aim in instructing should be to give users excellent skills rather than perfect ones.

Adult Learning

Adult learners in the academic library are likely to be college students (undergraduate and graduate), members of the faculty and staff of the institution, or citizens of the community who have been granted access to the library's resources. All of these individuals will have brought with them a broad range of experience with formal and informal education that has been tempered by their interactions in the "real world." In addition, adult learners enter the educational arena with the need to accomplish specific objectives. For them, training provides the tools to accomplish certain goals, it is not the goal in and of itself. For most adult learners, the goals include: training or retraining to gain employment; developing skills needed to keep or advance in the current job; or finding information that is relevant to their lives and problems. They come to libraries to find answers, and library training needs to be directed to that end. Therefore, adults must see the relevant applications of the training to the goals they wish to accomplish.

All human beings have a variety of approaches to learning at their command. However, as people mature, they develop preferences for one approach over another. In general, young children learn best when presented with concrete examples that are built through experience to form a theoretical concept, in that way working from concrete to abstract. As people mature, they are increasingly able to deal with abstract and theoretical constructs, deriving concrete examples from the abstract. However, when in new learning situations, adults may have a preference for being introduced to new concepts through the use of concrete examples. Jerold W. Apps has identified three major styles in which adult learners like to process the information they receive: intuitively, sequentially, and practically.[9] Intuitive learners like to "jump to their own conclusions," they like experiences that engage both their intellect and their emotions, and they like to have control over what they learn and how they apply it. Sequential learners prefer a more structured learning environment; they like to know what they are expected to learn and how they will be expected to apply it. Practical learners are interested in the end result of the learning as it applies directly to their real-life needs; they want immediate application and have little interest in theoretical matters.

Adults also have preferences for the way in which material is presented. Some adults learn most comfortably when the material is presented visually, others prefer to receive the information through auditory channels, and still others prefer to use their kinesthetic senses. Each of these preferred ways of learning can be accommodated in library instruction programs: reading lists, bibliographies, and case studies can be supplied for those who like to "read more about it"; lectures, discussions, interviews, and debates can be presented to help auditory learners become comfortable with new material; demonstrations and field trips are useful for those who like to see examples of what they are learning; and interactive computer programs, simulations, and hands-on experimentation work well for those who want to learn by doing. The teaching of adults ideally should be conducted so that the material is available visually, auditorily, and interactively, if possible.

Because adults are self-motivated and self-directed in learning situations, they learn best when given responsibility for their own learning. In this regard, we need to give them the opportunity to set their own goals, to be partners in the assessment of their progress, and, where feasible, to set their own timetables for mastery. Adults expect to be treated with respect in the learning environment, and expect the trainer to accept their goals and motivations for learning. Finally, adults are not shy about directing their own learning. They will take breaks when it fits their needs, not when prescribed by the trainer; they will interrupt to get answers whether they have been invited to do so or not; and they will not suffer fools gladly or poor teaching quietly.

In developing training for independent use of information resources, libraries should keep in mind the characteristics of adult learners. In fact, all training should be designed for adult learners. Undergraduate students, especially freshmen and sophomores, may not be as assertive as graduate students or faculty about their preferred learning styles. However, training should be designed to accommodate this diversity. This will greatly enhance the quality of the training offered, because it will be aimed at the most discerning audience.

Library training for adult learners should contain an inherent reward structure, one that allows the learners to independently assess their progress or success. The training should be structured in modules so that it can be consumed in separate learning sessions that fit into the schedules of adults who rarely can devote large blocks of time to such learning. The training should identify useful prior experience for each module or have a "preparatory" lesson so that all members of the group are in about the same place on the learning curve. Within each of the training modules, as well as between them, we should create "landmarks" that allow progress to be observed by the learner. Finally, the training should allow for modeling the skills to be learned, wherever possible.

In summary, training for adults should be hands on; flexibly paced; and have concrete, context-centered exercises and a theoretical framework.

Training Internal, External, and Eternal Customers

Training adults to access information resources independently requires a combination of human, technical, and conceptual skills. People should always take precedence in any training environment. The increase in "remote" users, combined with the increased diversity of the user population and the varying levels of systems expertise that users bring to a training session, presents challenges to the trainer. Nevertheless, the ability to communicate intelligently with users at varying levels of expertise is imperative, and possible. As we librarians learn, we need to train each other and the support staff, as well as end users. Training both trainers and users involves similar approaches. Some selected techniques, both conceptual and concrete, that have proved useful are outlined below.

Selected Training Techniques

• Assume nothing. In planning an introductory course or lesson, assume no knowledge on the part of the learners. It is helpful to query learners to determine their level of knowledge and/or their backgrounds. This may provide the trainer(s) with critical information on how to further customize the training.

• Decide what the goals and objectives of the training program are. What do you want your learners to be able to do? Be very specific. Your objectives will determine the content and the level of detail for your training session. After these are articulated, it is possible to effectively design the opening, the closing, and the body of your presentation.[10]

• Keep it simple. The training you are providing may be simple, but there is nothing more intolerable in a learning situation than simple ideas presented in a complex manner. Learn to present information incrementally. Even complex ideas are best mastered in simple steps.

• Maintain a focus. Do not introduce extraneous concepts. Introduce only those concepts relevant to the subject at hand. Again, keep it simple.

• Be open to sharing information. Adult learners are not interested in "power trips." The most effective trainers do not engage in "turf wars." Training for autonomy in the use of electronic resources requires the sharing of human resources (i.e., some learners may have as much or more experience with technology as the trainer and may also help less experienced learners). All trainers should be actively engaged in teaching.

• Motivating participants is an important strategy for effective learning. "One of the best ways to motivate is to stress the relevance of the training for the attendees."[11]

• Trainers must remain flexible, actively listening to the real needs of the trainee(s). There is no single, formulaic approach to training or learning.

• Actively listening to trainees' questions is different from simply hearing their questions. Listen to both the messages and the metamessages.[12] Ask yourself: "What do they really want?"

• Offer nonjudgmental learning. Grading, in any form is *not* conducive to an adult learning environment, nor is it most effective in anyone's learning process.

• Teach in layers, in ever-increasing detail. Utilizing this layered approach, like peeling layers of an onion, respects the diversity and experience of the individual learners.

• Repeat the most salient points. Human beings absorb information in differing degrees. Repetition creates the most effective "hit rate," and is a key aspect to the layered approach to training. In short: Tell them what you are going to tell them. Tell them. Tell them what you have told them.

• Standardize basic training so that everyone has the same foundational level from the beginning, then provide customized one-on-one instruction. This is another key aspect to the layered approach of training.[13]

• The concept of teams is useful for both learners and trainers. The learner's participation is vital. Treating the learner as part of a team can be most effective in vesting interest in the learning situation. The team concept provides for a unity of purpose. "Purpose is a consciously chosen and clearly articulated direction which uses the talents and abilities of your team, contributes to the organization, and leads to a sense of fulfillment for the team members."[14] Team teaching can also be an effective style for group learning. Effective training is often enhanced when material is presented from different perspectives.

• One-on-one instruction may be appropriate in some cases. The person-to-person interaction provides the most direct and immediate feedback and thus facilitates greater retention. Individual attention and focus let the learner know that this training is important.

• Cramped quarters and other environmental distractions are not helpful for either trainers or learners. Respecting the human need for a reasonably comfortable learning environment can dramatically improve students' retention of the material.

• Provide concrete examples from the learner's personal experience. Concrete, context-centered examples and exercises facilitate learning, through involvement and understanding. Use as many visual aids as possible to help make the ideas real. There are many diverse learning styles, including abstract to concrete and concrete to abstract. Visual aids are a method of optimizing the different learning styles.

• In each session, bring the learner(s) to a saturation point but do not overkill. There are limits to the amount of information any individual can absorb.

• Actively learn from your teaching/training experiences. Continuous improvement as a trainer is the result of evaluation and analysis of each training session.

• Training and learning should be fun. Add a timely dash of humor. Who said that instruction must always be presented in a serious manner? Humor has been found to enhance memory for learning.

• Learn to laugh about your own training mistakes during the session. There is nothing more human than to be able to laugh about ourselves.

Conclusion

Although we may find teaching users to become independent a great challenge, it is also very rewarding. The challenge is to adapt to a great variety of learning styles, cultural backgrounds, and personalities among students. As good teachers, we must stay abreast of rapidly changing systems and sources. Our reward is in knowing that we are contributing to information literacy. This is essential if our users are going to learn how to learn. Teaching information literacy is something that we are well qualified to do, and it is the most important service we can provide to our users.

Notes

1. S. Michael Malinconico, "Technology and the Academic Workplace," *Library Administration & Management* 5 (winter 1991): 25.

2. Carla Stoffle, "The Upside of Downsizing: Using the Economic Crisis to Restructure and Revitalize Academic Libraries," in *The Upside of Downsizing: Using Library Instruction to Cope*, ed. Cheryl LaGuardia, Stella Bentley, and Janet Martorana, (New York: Neal-Schumann, 1995), 9.

3. Ibid., 8.

4. Malinconico, "Technology and the Academic Workplace," 26.

5. Lizabeth A. Wilson, "Instruction as a Reference Source," in *Reference and Information Services: An Introduction*, 2nd ed., ed. Richard E. Bopp and Linda C. Smith, (Englewood, Colo.: Libraries Unlimited, 1995) 153.

6. Thomas Kirk, "Course-Related Library Instruction in the 70's," in *Library Instruction in the Seventies: State of the Art*, ed. Hannelore B. Rader (Ann Arbor, Mich.: Pierian, 1977), 40.

7. See, for example, *Bibliographic Instruction and the Learning Process: Theory, Style and Motivation*, ed. Carolyn A. Kirkendall (Ann Arbor, Mich.: Pierian, 1984); *Bibliographic Instruction: The Second Generation*, ed. Constance A. Mellon (Littleton, Colo.: Libraries Unlimited, 1987); *Conceptual Frameworks for Bibliographic Education: Theory into Practice*, ed. Mary Reichel and Mary Ann Ramey (Littleton, Colo.: Libraries Unlimited, 1987).

8. Lori Arp, "An Introduction to Learning Theory," in *Sourcebook for Bibliographic Instruction*, ed. Katherine Branch (Chicago: ACRL, 1993), 5–6.

9. Jerold W. Apps, *Mastering the Teaching of Adults* (Malabar, Fla.: Krieger, 1991).

10. For an excellent introduction concerning presentations, see David A. Peoples, *Presentations Plus: David Peoples Proven Techniques*, 2d ed. (New York: Wiley, 1992).

11. Stephanie C. Ardito, *Customer Services and User Training* (Philadelphia: National Federation of Abstracting and Information Services, 1991), 62.

12. For a discussion on conversational style and meaning, see Deborah Tannen, *That's Not What I Meant!: How Conversational Style Makes or Breaks Relationships* (New York: Ballantine, 1987).

13. Stephen J. Smith, "Cataloging with Copy: Methods for Increasing Productivity," *Technical Services Quarterly* 11, no. 4 (1994): 8–9.

14. Steve Buchholz and Thomas Roth, *Creating the High Performance Team* (New York: Wiley, 1987), 54.

Service-Oriented Personnel

Patricia A. McCandless

> Therefore, the Sage administers without action
> and instructs without words.
> He lets all things rise without dominating them,
> produces without attempting to possess,
> acts without asserting,
> achieves without taking credit.[1]

Michael Gorman argues that a "service attitude" must come from the top and that management is to blame for negative attitudes. Working with employees to provide high-quality, timely service to users is an art. Responsive, creative service is developed and nurtured by managers who hire the right people, manage them effectively, and give them latitude to try new approaches. Good management of people is key to risk-taking and open questioning of the status quo. Focusing on recent trends in library service, this chapter gives particular attention to the adaptation of management theories from the business world. It discusses the changing characteristics of the work force and the attributes of effective managers in this new environment. The chapter concludes with some basic, practical pointers for supporting employees to achieve personal and library goals for better service to users.

Until the late 1970s, academic libraries assumed that they had a captive, stable user population already committed to education and

142

lifelong learning. Consequently, these libraries, on the whole, did not focus on user services with the zeal of public and special libraries. But as the number of institutions of higher education increased and the numbers of traditional students began to decline, competition for students became an institutional reality. Academic libraries, in concert with their universities, began to emulate the business sector. This phenomenon has paralleled the rise of consumer rights and expectations. These trends and the public's unrest with education at all levels has caused colleges and universities and their libraries to reexamine all facets of their service operation.[2]

Before these changes in higher education occurred, libraries had grown in size and complexity. They became bureaucratic organizations where work was broken into specific tasks based on functionality and standardization was the mode of operation. The growth of bibliographic utilities and turnkey automated systems had further standardized library operations.[3] As functional bureaucracies, libraries have developed units where "the work focuses on specialized parts of the operation rather than the whole and control comes in the form of detailed reports of time and resources expended, and managers rely more on information systems and less on personal contact."[4] Bureaucracies place greater attention on the process than on outcomes. Managers "have a strong incentive to worry more about constraints than tasks. . . . It is hard to hold managers accountable for attaining a goal, easy to hold them accountable for conforming to the rules."[5] "The standard systems used in most organizations debase the human spirit and rob individuals of their own self-worth. We do it in a hundred different ways."[6] In such organizations, equity is often more important than either efficiency or effectiveness; and managers, as well as workers, are less inclined to be risk takers. Bureaucracies tend to develop rules to ensure that constraints are not violated so that little action at all is possible because every action must conform to a rule. Such organizations call for more managers to ensure that rules and constraints are adhered to. The only discretion is held by upper management, those who are farthest from the daily operation.[7]

However, the 1970s witnessed a growth of professionalism within libraries and its attendant tension with hierarchical administrative structures.[8] These professionals chafed against bureaucracy and wanted more authority over their work to achieve a greater sense of responsibility, achievement, and personal development. They sought variety, a vertical expansion of their job duties, and the autonomy to accomplish their work without conforming to certain prescribed processes. They want to achieve the end result with little interference from their supervisor. Unlike their predecessors, this new generation of professionals placed their loyalty with the profession and professional advancement rather than to the organization. They were willing to forego other benefits for job quality because of their strong individual identity and interest in the quality of their life. However, many organizations, including libraries, often "operate in ways that are in conflict with those characteristics by formalizing roles, relationships, and procedures."[9]

One manifestation of the growth of professionalism has been the demand by librarians to be stakeholders in the library's administration through participatory management, often embodied in organizational constitutions and bylaws and in committees to conduct the library's business, including committees that participate in the hiring process. However, librarian participation generally has been restricted and librarians have been given little or no control over day-to-day operations or the budget.

Strained budgets and technological change have resulted in a downward shift of tasks from librarians to staff, with paraprofessional staff now in the throes of professionalism experienced by librarians in the 1970s, and, more recently, a greater reliance on student assistants with a concomitant downward shifting of more clerical duties to the lowest level. As resources available to libraries declined, and efforts to reduce duplication in collections and utilize staff in other areas grew, branch/department libraries have been consolidated, and undergraduate libraries, in particular, closed. Librarians and staff feel overworked and undervalued.

Management Trends

If the unrest and dissatisfaction among librarians were not enough, libraries, as well as all of higher education, are being pressured to become more cost-effective, thereby creating a conflict of service provision and efficiency. To cope with these pressures, libraries began to embrace management techniques and programs utilized by private business to capture users and provide high-quality service. Long-range planning, management by objectives (MBO), organization development (OD), total quality management (TQM), continuing quality improvement (CQI), and reengineering are but a few of the more recent tools brought from the business world to service and public organizations.[10] However, libraries, although able to achieve efficiencies by using business techniques, are not businesses that offer products for sale at a profit. Libraries, by their very nature, cannot be cost-effective because they do not sell services. Therefore, applying business management techniques to libraries is questionable in light of the disparate missions of the two types of organizations. Service organizations, in particular, often fall into the trap of confusing efficiency with effectiveness. As a profession, we know little about our users' expectations as we design services and systems. Research on user needs and expectations would help libraries plan new services. Accountability and wise use of resources should be in step with college and university missions, and all units must ensure that user needs are being met and exceeded if we hope to remain a viable information provider. Those ends can be met outside the theories of the business world.

In an attempt to meet the challenges of the declining purchasing power for higher education, libraries have been flattening the organizational structure, a response borrowed from the corporate world. Joseph A. Raelin notes that successful large organizations may recognize and accommodate professionals' autonomy by flattening the organization and permitting a mixture of operation/ organization within departments.[11] However, the configurations we are seeing in libraries are functional in nature rather than user centered. Permitting librarians and staff the latitude of planning and executing broad areas of responsibility may, in fact, perpetuate the barriers to communication and service that currently exist. Although ostensibly designed to embody participatory management, they place more authority at the top of the organization rather than pushing it downward. The continued micro division of labor underutilizes people.

Management Failure

Libraries have experienced these management fads with little assessment or real commitment to them. Although these strategies are not necessarily well suited to academic libraries, they are popular and often imposed from above, thus forcing libraries to make the best of them. Changes resulting from implementation of management theories are often short term, and people do not realize that change demands constant work and commitment. "Most research shows positive evidence for short-term change in behavior resulting from management training; however, there is less evidence to support claims of permanent changes in behavior. The change that occurs most readily from training is the acquisition of human relations attitudes."[12] Leadership and management practices change too often. One major factor in the disenchantment people have with various management programs is that participants are unaware of the time and effort that must be expended at every level of the organization before any desired outcomes are apparent.[13] No matter what program a library undertakes— whether MBO, strategic planning, or TQM—it must be embraced by top administration. Too many ventures have failed because administration gave lip service to a program but then exhibited behavior that showed a lack of commitment and action. It is impossible to engage the entire organization if top administration either is not committed or is giving mixed signals. "The most predictable thing about organizational innovation is the likelihood of executive rationality being surprised and even confounded by the depth of feeling and the unimagined misunderstandings which it provokes."[14] Complacency is an easy, but destructive, force. "What we term 'hard' systems management methodology is the most sophisticated and comprehensive form of 'scientific' management. . . . Hard systems perspectives assume that virtually all organizational realities are capable of being precisely defined, tightly structured, quantified and measured. It assumes that organization members can be readily trained and induced to respond accurately and reliably to complex procedures, and can do so without stress and alienation. It also assumes that all staff share a common perception of organizational realities (which tends in effect to be that of senior management) and can be relied upon to behave at all times in a rational and calculative fashion."[15]

Management Success

Good management practice makes good user service possible. Successful management requires the involvement of the library staff in planning for change. Change is necessary, but there are pitfalls. A staff that spends hours every week in meetings to plan organizational change has little energy left to serve the public. Given the conflicting pressures on staff time, planning needs to be efficient as well as effective. Henry Mintzberg pointed out some of the hazards of traditional planning procedures:

> Conventional planning tends to be a conservative process, sometimes encouraging behavior that undermines both creativity and strategic thinking. It can be inflexible, breeding resistance to major strategic change and discouraging truly novel ideas in favor of extrapolation of the status quo or marginal adaptation, ultimately, therefore, focusing attention on the short term rather than the long term. . . . internal political climate considered so antithetical to planning can sometimes help to foster strategic change in organizations, while planning itself can sometimes foster dysfunctional political activity...a climate congenial to planning can *sometimes* be antithetical to effective strategy making, and so the "right" climate can sometimes be hostile to planning.[16]

Managers should be cognizant of these factors and work to ensure that such feelings and misunderstandings are addressed and that the new direction is constantly discussed and actions measured against that framework. There must be adequate resources to support a changed environment. The manager's job, which should focus more on results than on process, is developmental by detailing and providing those resources and coordinating their use. Yet, the successful organization must constantly be changing, fine-tuning, scrutinizing its operations to ensure that services provided are what users want.

"Three of the key elements in the art of working together are how to deal with change, how to deal with conflict, and how to reach our potential."[17] Successful organizations "combine high levels of central control with substantial decentralization, autonomy, and entrepreneurship. They maintain control mostly through values and cultures rather than relying on procedures and systems."[18] Healthy organizations are characterized by "effective task accomplishment, internal integration (optimal use of human resources, high morale and a clear and attractive organizational identity) and capacity for change and growth."[19]

Not all management practices are faddish. Some, like the ones just described, are part of a core of management theory that runs through much of management literature. The role of the manager becomes more complex as libraries shift from paternalistic, authoritarian organizations to a participatory model where employees are no longer over managed.

> The post-bureaucratic paradigm values argumentation and deliberation about how the roles of public managers should be framed. Informed public managers today understand and appreciate such varied role concepts as exercising leadership, creating an uplifting mission and organizational culture, strategic planning, managing without direct authority, pathfinding, problem setting, identifying customers, groping along, reflecting in action, coaching, structuring incentives, changing products, instilling commitment to quality, creating a climate for innovation, building teams, redesigning work, investing in people, negotiating mandates, and managing by walking around.[20]

> The style of participative management is at its best when the supervisor can draw out the best in his people, allow decisions to be made at the point of influence and contribution, and create a spirit that everyone is in it together and that if something is unknown, they'll learn it together. There are also times when the appropriate style is one of laissez-faire management, which permits the staff to work on its own without interference. Finally, there are also times, though infrequently, when the supervisor must be very directive about goals and purpose. Participative

management has been shown to be by far the most effective leadership style, particularly in building motivation and stimulating progress toward organizational goals.[21]

Likert found that employee-centered managers were more effective than task-centered managers.[22] "The best managers, and there are many, are those who understand time, feeling, and focus and have the ability to make their vision and mission real to others in such a natural way that doing so appears effortless."[23] Some specific examples of these "commonsense" approaches to working with people in the postbureaucratic model follow.

Managing Service-oriented Staff

Gorman described the seven deadly sins of service as apathy, brush-off, coldness, condescension, robotism, rule book, and runaround. How can mangers create a working environment that discourages these negative behaviors? To begin with, they need to know what is going on in the library. Valid in any environment is the walk-around manager. Managers need to be cognizant of the actual workplace as well as statistical reports. Employees resent managers who visit them in their unit only once a year or only once in the manager's lifetime. People are pleased to be able to show their accomplishments and talk about their goals and perceived barriers. They need a relaxed forum for lobbying. The manager should know and speak with all the staff, even get to know some of the student assistants. Much can be learned from impromptu site visits, and confidence and trust can mutually be developed. Ideas and suggestions that might never be raised in a formal setting can be brought forward in a more open and relaxed environment. After a strong working relationship is established, people will feel comfortable raising issues in formal settings as well. Heated discussions and give-and-take are healthy as long as discussion revolves around ideas and not personalities. Disagreement can stimulate critical thinking and is necessary for a healthy organization, so managers must be willing to be challenged. In addition to walking around, managers should be accessible and maintain an open-door policy. It is also important to be responsive. If no immediate response to a query can be made, the reply should at least be timely.

Many organizations, especially bureaucratic ones, respond to trimming or living within their budgets by making small cuts such as restricting phone calls and the number of telephones, cutting back on supplies and small equipment, regulating breaks, etc. When people are feeling stress and uncertainty, a heavy hand with such inexpensive essentials leads to poor morale and anger. People will be non-productive while they complain bitterly about such petty economies, and they will find ways to retaliate. When people perceive times to be lean and uncertain, managers should find ways of praising and rewarding good performance and ensuring some socializing to send a message that administration is aware of people's stress and potential feelings of alienation and being undervalued. Some very reasonable, yet fairly inexpensive, ways of rewarding people range the gamut from providing opportunities for people to showcase their current activities to others in the library or on campus to formal recognition of outstanding work with certificates, plaques, money, or other perks. Support for continuing education and participation in professional organizations, including disciplined-based bodies outside the field of librarianship, enhance people's quality of life and professional well-being. Allowing an employee to take advantage of an invitation to serve occasionally as a consultant bolsters that individual's sense of being valued.

It is important to hire the right individual for each job. Employees should have intellectual curiosity, a willingness to learn, analytical skills, affinity for change to the point of devising change for change sake, an abhorrence for the routine, the ability to question the status quo and to see different sides of an issue. The corporate world does engage in personality testing for its leaders; and libraries, too, could benefit from being cognizant of employee traits revealed by the Myers-Briggs Type Indicator. Libraries today can ill afford to hire people who perform best in structured situations and believe they know best what users need. Rather, libraries need people who see their service mission as more important than other tasks. Anyone not stimulated and challenged by change and willing to adapt should not consider a career in librarianship. However, libraries should not make the mistake of filling the ranks with people of the same temperament but, rather, should ensure a balance of personal styles to gain benefit from different points of view. Especially for senior positions, libraries should actively recruit by following the pattern of athletic and some academic departments by always maintaining a short list of potential candidates for vacancies.

Some enlightened managers are beginning to question the ritual of annual performance appraisals as causing more angst for both parties than achieving any positive outcome. Performance feedback should be ongoing and occur at the point of action, not just at annual review for salary increases. Constructive criticism is an oxymoron because people focus on the negative and ignore the positive and any suggestions for change. One manager goes as far as suggesting never criticizing for anything because people are so self-critical they will bring up the negative themselves, thereby opening the door for discussion.[24] Because the old adage about catching more flies with honey than with vinegar holds true even today, managers should offer praise and encouragement. Criticism stops behavior, whereas praise encourages behavior. Any improvement or positive change should be so acknowledged. Counseling and coaching are a large part of managers' responsibilities, especially discussion of how better reactions or solutions could be applied in the future to similar situations. Formal evaluations should be based on outcomes, not on the process. Even so, over time performance ratings tend to become unreliable. Managers grow to expect more than they did initially or become complacent and do not challenge people to strive for better performance. Managers should work positively on changing some behavior by being selective and not trying to transform people or organizations overnight.

Managers should recognize and appreciate personalities and styles different from their own, and learn to distinguish between substance and style.

> Because of contextuality, the performance of any single element depends heavily on its degree of fit with its context. It means that individual people can perform way above or below what appears to be their individual potential, depending on the degree and kind of support they get from the surrounding system. It means that individual performance will be intensely conscious of the kind and degree of surrounding support. It means that

parts cannot be exchanged like chess pieces; transfers in
and out of people, replacements of equipment, and so on
are felt intensely.[25]

Some people in any organization do their thinking aloud, whereas
others conduct their personal dialogues internally. Those who need to
vocalize their ideas and weigh the pros and cons out loud need a willing,
sympathetic ear. Failure to listen to them will result in their poor
morale; and they will bend someone's ear and probably complain about
the uncaring, automaton administration. Giving them latitude to
verbalize their thoughts and feelings will instill a sense of well-being
that will make them an effective and supportive member of the
organization. These people need a lot of attention, but they are often
innovators and among the best employees. Others may need more
autonomy to direct and achieve their work. "Giants give others the gift
of space, space in both the personal and the corporate sense, space to be
what one can be."[26] The manager should be supportive, periodically
check progress, provide resources to permit success, and ensure that any
needed coordination occurs.

People need to sense that their feelings are taken seriously, so
expressing empathy is a must for a manager. Even a heated discussion
can be tolerable if both parties can truthfully say, "I understand how you
feel." Expressions of empathy also help dissolve anger and frustration
should those emotions come into play.

Not asking others to do something you would not do yourself is a
way of cautioning managers from climbing into the ivory tower.
Employees are more responsive to managers who empathize with them
and are viewed as part of the work process rather than isolated and out
of touch. Managers who occasionally perform some staff tasks send a
signal that work is a group process. Doing staff work also enables the
manager to understand better the conditions the employees face daily.
However, although doing occasional staff work is valuable, managers
should guard against abandoning their role as the manager and slipping
into the routine of doing others' work.

It is important to get several points of view. The emperor who
wore no clothes suffered humiliation by surrounding himself with
sycophants who were unwilling to convey the truth, an easy trap to fall

into. Any issue probably has as many viewpoints as there are people, so the wise manager tries to get advice from all parties involved before proceeding. Managers should try to establish a climate where people feel unthreatened by their honesty and give accurate feedback. Trust must be established so people are willing to express themselves freely, take risks, and share. On major issues where there may be divided opinions, managers should clearly explain the rationale that led to a particular outcome. They should try to build consensus and be cognizant of all those who need to be consulted to ensure that all issues have been raised and evaluated by those directly affected. Networking and building coalitions can overcome resistance. Managers can plant seeds for action while listening and focusing on interests, not positions. They should try to find solutions that are better for all parties.[27] They need to be flexible and willing to change course if circumstance or changed conditions dictate. One should have convictions and trust one's own instincts but not become intransigent.

"One of the key problems facing American organizations...is that they are underled and overmanaged. They do not pay enough attention to doing the right thing, while they pay too much attention to doing things right."[28] Policies should be general guidelines that give employees the latitude to interpret them based on the specifics of a situation. The commitment to outstanding service must pervade the entire organization so that every employee has the latitude to do the "right thing" in any given situation. One should never create policies to address a small percentage of occurrences, thereby making everyone suffer for a small number of problem instances.

Managers should support initiative and encourage entrepreneurship verbally, as well as with tangible rewards. Merit salary raises, rather than across the board, allow the manager to reward such initiative. Professionals are creative and have entrepreneurial instincts that need to be nurtured. The manager's role is to provide resources and support and to ensure integration among relevant operating units. Entrepreneurship must be supported by allowing individuals to formulate their own projects, implement them, and work without day-to-day supervision. Managers need to support risk-taking and be willing to accept any changes such entrepreneurship may bring. Failure must also be supported without placing blame if risk-taking is to continue.[29] Continuous needs assessment and surveying, especially in light of remote user and self-service needs, support such initiative. Professional leaves for research and retooling, job rotation, or job exchanges within the library or across institutions stimulate professional growth and initiative. Managers should promote and reclassify positions as they evolve.

Conclusion

Managers empower librarians and staff to be service oriented. Employees who feel that their work is unappreciated or misunderstood become robots expending the least effort possible. Those whose ideas are dismissed or ignored become apathetic. Rule book, runaround, and brush-off are the refuge of employees who are not given enough training or positive reinforcement for risk-taking. Condescension and coldness are attitudes transferred from the top down. Managers can not dictate a service attitude, but they can hire the right person for the job. They can know the work of their fellow employees, listen to their problem, and help to find solutions. They can also reward employees who provide good service.

They can lead in developing routines, policies, and programs that focus on user needs, not make the work more convenient or predictable for employees. Managers can, by example, set the tone for expectations within the work environment.

Management is not an end. For the library, it is the means to create high-quality service. There is no single best way to mange a library, but common threads run through good management. To meet changing service needs of uses, libraries need management that is dynamic and practical rather than static, always moving forward rather than maintaining equilibrium. Like all artistry, the best management appears effortless and easy to emulate.

Notes

1. Lao-tzu, *A Translation of Lao Tzu's Tao te Ching and Wang Pi's Commentary*, trans. Paul J. Lin (Ann Arbor, Mich.: Center for Chinese Studies, University of Michigan, 1977): book 1, chapter 2.

2. Daniel T. Seymour, *On Q: Causing Quality in Higher Education* (New York: American Council on Education/Macmillan, 1992), presents an interesting view of higher education.

3. James Q. Wilson, *Bureaucracy: What Government Agencies Do and Why They Do It* (New York: Basic Bks., 1989), gives a good overview of bureaucracy in the public sector.

4. Joseph A. Raelin, *The Clash of Cultures: Managers and Professionals* (Boston: Harvard Business School Pr., 1986), 59–60.

5. Wilson, *Bureaucracy*, 131.

6. Seymour, *On Q*, 114.

7. Wilson, *Bureaucracy*, 133.

8. Raelin, *The Clash of Cultures*, traces the rise of professionalism, its characteristics, and the failure of traditional management practices in dealing with the professional employee. Ken Jones, *Conflict and Change in Library Organizations: People, Power and Service* (London: Clive Bingley, 1984), traces the history of "hard" management theories and argues in favor of a new, "softer" approach to enable library organizations to provide relevant service to users.

9. Ibid., 7.

10. For a longer discussion of recent management fads, see Allen B. Veaner, "Paradigm Lost, Paradigm Regained? A Persistent Personnel Issue in Academic Librarianship, II" *College & Research Libraries* 55 (Sept. 1994): 389–402.

11. Raelin, *The Clash of Cultures*, 21.

12. Michael Nash, *Making People Productive* (San Francisco: Jossey-Bass, 1985), 85.

13. Lee G. Bolman and Terrance E. Deal, *Reframing Organizations: Artistry, Choice, and Leadership* (San Francisco: Jossey-Bass, 1991); Jones, *Conflict and Chnage in Library Organizations*; Henry Mintzberg, *The Rise and Fall of Strategic Planning: Reconceiving Roles for Planning, Plans, Planners* (New York: Free Pr., 1994); and Raelin provide sound assessment of various management theories.

14. Jones, *Conflict and Change in Library Organizations*, 216.

15. Ibid., 69.

16. Mintzberg, *The Rise and Fall of Strategic Planning*, 158.

17. Max DePree, *Leadership Is an Art* (New York: Dell, 1989), 54.

18. Bolman and Deal, *Reforming Organizations*, 334.

19. Edwin E. Olson, "Relation of Information Use, Organizational Factors and Technological Innovation: A Presentation of Research Results," *Aslib Proceedings* 29 (Jan. 1977): 6.

20. Michael Barzelay, *Breaking through Bureaucracy: A New Vision for Managing in Government* (Berkely: Univ. of California Pr., 1992), 132.

21. Raelin, *The Clash of Cultures*, 208.

22. Bolman and Deal, *Reforming Organizations*, 141.

23. Peter B. Vaill, *Managing as a Performing Art: New Ideas for a World of Chaotic Change* (San Francisco: Jossey-Bass, 1989), 170.

24. Nash, *Making People Productive*, 156.

25. Vaill, *Managing as a Performing Art*, 122.

26. DePree, *Leadership is an Art*, 75.

27. Bolman and Deal, *Reforming Organizations*, 208–10.

28. Warren Bennis, "The 4 Competencies of Leadership," *Training & Development Journal* 38 (Aug. 1984): 16–17.

29. Raelin, *The Clash of Cultures*, 73.

It's Only Money:
Financial Resources in the
User-Centered Library

Dale S. Montanelli

It is absolutely true that resources must be provided . . . . It
is not a question of providing funds with the implication of
more funds; it may be a question of reallocation both of
funds and, certainly, time.[1]

Although some of the best things in life are free, libraries are not
among them. Because the cost of academic libraries is generally
hidden from them, users fail to understand the way in which budgetary
choices directly affect service. Of the resources available to libraries—
people, money, and space—only money has real flexibility. In most colleges and universities, space is fairly constant, especially for libraries
with their extraordinary floor load-bearing requirements. People also
tend to be stable resources, although in cases of high levels of staff
turnover hiring, and training replacements can consume vast amounts
of resources. The only thing that can change without warning is the
amount of money available to meet library needs. Legislatures may
appropriate more or less, university administrations may allocate more
or less, without a clear understanding of the consequences of such decisions on the day-to-day operations of the library. Even within the
library, decisions to shift emphases may change the resources available
to a particular division. For example, a shift in allocation away from the
circulation department may result in decreased stack maintenance.

Historically, libraries have had to fight for adequate financial resources. During a brief time in the 1960s, higher education in general and libraries in particular enjoyed a period of financial growth.[2] However, by the 1970s and 1980s, the cost of running libraries increased at a more rapid rate than general inflation. Although there was growth in absolute dollars, libraries lost purchasing power.[3] The Association of College and Research Libraries, Standards for College Libraries 1986, recommended that the library receive six percent of the total institutional budget for educational and general purposes, yet since 1949, the highest this percentage has been for academic libraries was 4.1 percent in 1970; and in recent years, there has been a steady decline in the library's share of the institution's resources.[4] Accompanying this decline has been an increased emphasis on accountability for how the funds are used.

Because current financial pressures throughout academia, not just the library, have strained available financial resources, faculty have become even more concerned and excitable about the library's resources and competition for a share of these resources has developed among different disciplines. The inability to purchase new books and journals and the extensive cancellation of journal subscriptions have been viewed as assaults on scholarly endeavors. At the same time, students and their advocates have resented the portion of the budget spent on esoteric materials. In this context, how the library makes decisions about its financial resources is very important. A library in which people come first approaches resource-allocation decisions in an open and consultative fashion. This may require planning for the library in a different way and on a different timetable than is used in the parent institution, even though the parent institution's deadlines and formats must be met.

The user-centered library will involve faculty, students, and library staff in its priority setting. Entering such a consultative process is not for the faint of heart. The process of asking for input often establishes a belief on the part of those providing the advice that the advice will be taken. However, the campus administration, the faculty, the students, and the staff of the library see the library from vastly different perspectives and advice given by one group can (and often does) contradict the advice given by another.[5] There are many ways to solicit input concerning the library's priorities: surveys, focus groups, and faculty advisory committees. However, most of these techniques leave each group without experience of the opinions of the other groups. When one group's advice leads to policies opposed by another group, the latter may well become frustrated with the library. One possible solution to this dilemma is to bring together all of the "stakeholders" (faculty, students, library staff, administrators, etc.) in a process called *Future Search*.[6] This process, an intensive three-day program, brings perceived stakeholders together to determine what they can agree upon as common ground. By starting with those things all stakeholders can agree to, it becomes possible for the library to build a mission and specific goals that will find "buy-in" from the various constituent groups. It is a process well worth the time for any library intent on developing new directions for the future. It is a crucial process for libraries that need to rebuild the loyalty of constituents and at the same time move in new directions.

Financial Management Tools
Mission and Goals of the Library
The budget planning process does not start with the dollar resources available but, rather, with the mission and goals of the library. Getting the mission right is the most important step. In *The Seven Habits of Highly Effective People*, Stephen Covey described the experience of working very hard to climb a ladder, but of being so busy climbing the ladder that one does not ask the question, "Is the ladder against the correct wall?"[7] The same question may be asked of the budget development process in the libraries. The allocation may be consultative, it may be widely communicated, but if the allocation process does not provide resources for the institution's highest priorities, it will not meet the needs of the patrons or the library staff. Therefore, the first step in the process of building the budget is the development of a mission statement and goals for the library. (See Prentice,[8] Daubert,[9] and Talbot.[10]) The library must be able to establish its priorities before it can allocate resources. As Murray S. Martin has pointed out:

> The difference between decisions on policy and decisions on money is often misunderstood. In general, the budget

reflects policy decisions by trying to ensure that the amounts and the distribution of available money will match the needs of the various programs which result from the decisions on policy.[11]

The creation of a budget is really the commitment in dollars to honor the priorities established.

> The profession also needs to be careful that finance does not become 'the tail that wags the dog.' . . . Finance is about managing and paying for the vision, but it is hoped it does not become the only model and vision in the end.[12]

In a library focused on users, it is important to involve the people served as well as the people who work in the library in the development of the mission and later in the development of the specific goals for the year or years ahead.

Allowing the stakeholders to agree on common ground is the first step in developing a mission statement, but ongoing consultation is also needed. The appointment of an advisory committee consisting of faculty, student, and library representatives is one way to obtain this input. The library's director may chair this committee, and its chief financial officer may serve ex officio. This committee can help in the establishment of the mission and the development of goals related to the mission. Its members also can disseminate information to the rest of the campus and can act as advocates for the library with the campus administration. Interaction with campus groups also assists the library director and financial officer to understand user priorities and the extent to which these priorities carry intellectual and emotional baggage. Although some library directors and some librarians feel that consultation diminishes control, the library's best allies on the campus are those who have developed understanding through full communication.

Budget Planning
Budget planning is the process of turning the library goals into action steps and assigning a price tag to each of these action steps. The action

steps should be concrete services or activities the library wishes to perform in the year for which the budget is being developed. Determining the price of an activity or service requires the gathering of data. The data are gathered for the purpose of determining the cost of each library activity or service.

> Knowledge of the true costs of library functions ensures that the LIS manager is able to consider alternative means of supplying the service required. Such knowledge also allows the funding management to be convinced that the unit is providing value for the money . . . . The finished output of a costing exercise will be clear, detailed and timely information.[13]

The data in large part may come from statistics the library is already gathering—circulation of various types of material, OPAC use, reference questions, etc.—or from decision documents of the library (minutes, memos, etc.). For information not easily gathered routinely in libraries, Ann E. Prentice describes methods for gathering cost information for library activities.[14] These techniques are particularly useful when trying to put a price tag on an activity the library has not previously provided. It is important in gathering data for cost analysis to create clearly defined units of measurement for the activity, ones that are countable and verifiable. As Prentice has stressed:

> An unsatisfactory means of allocating cost is to take the total expenditure of a department or unit for a year and divide by a unit of activity. The results of such a method are unuseable; there is no identification of variables only a lumping together of all costs divided by an available user figure . . . it is not possible to measure productivity from such poorly defined figures.[15]

After data are gathered and the cost of each service or activity has been accurately determined, the library is in the position to produce "the budget." Martin described the budget as:

an outward and visible sign of an inward and spiritual intent (apologies to the catechism) in that it objectifies a library's programs and gives them reality, even if that reality feels like a set of limits.[16]

A budget that ties the program to the funding provides a backbone around which the library activities occur and that provides a way of determining the price tags for various strategies to accomplish the library's goals.[17] The budget is the way of making real the priorities of the library (putting your money where your mouth is) and of later being able to assess progress toward those priorities. The budget becomes not just an accounting requirement but, rather, a necessary part of creative library management.[18]

Analysis of the costs of library services can be particularly helpful in explaining decisions to users. Users who are given concrete information about the cost of services and the trade-offs involved are more likely to buy into the library's budgetary decisions. For example, science faculty who are given the institutional price and cost per use of journals in their field (as compared to the faculty purchase price) are more likely to accept document delivery as opposed to ownership of those journals. Although this process does not remove library service decisions from the realm of the political, it should remove them from the realm of the emotional to that of the logical.

The exact form the budget takes is dependent on the requirements of the parent institution. Daubert[19] and Martin[20] both describe the six major types of budget methodologies in common use. These are: line-item budgeting, program budgeting, performance budgeting, the planning-programming-budgeting system, zero-based budgeting, and formula budgeting. Of these, the line-item budget and some variation of the program/performance budget are most commonly used by institutions of higher education. In the line-item model, the budget receives increments (in "good" budget years) based on the lines in the budget. These increments are often in the form of percentages against the total of the line. The most frequently found "lines" or "objects of expenditure" are likely to be: personnel, benefits, supplies, contractual services, equipment, and library materials. In this budget method, the human resource costs, the various expense categories, and the library materials are not tied to any particular service or activity. One consequence of this is that it is very easy to increase (or decrease) the library budget in a very mechanical way, with the changes (positive or negative) not related to the impacts they have on services and activities.

The program/performance budget models (including the planning-programming-budgeting system and zero-based budgeting) have one thing in common: they tie the budget to the activities and services performed. These budgets are typically grouped around functions, such as cataloging, reference, or circulation. But they may also be grouped around units of service such as the biology library or the OPAC. The program/performance budget for any given activity or service contains within it all of the costs for carrying out the activity or service. Although it may be presented as a "cost per item cataloged" or a "cost per transaction on the OPAC," these figures are built on an analysis that includes the personnel costs, the supply costs, the contractual services costs, and the equipment costs. Ideally, it would also include the "overhead" costs, which reflect the dollar value of the library administrative and support costs associated with the activity. This link, which allows the library to go from a program/performance budget model to a line-item budget model, is very important because it allows the library to operate internally in a program/performance budget model, even if the parent institution relies on a line-item budget structure.

The real value of the program/performance budget models (and why they tend to proliferate) is that they so clearly tie the goals and objectives of the library to precise dollar amounts. They provide a way for the library to determine the impact of decreased resources on activities and provide input for the hard decisions that have to be made in such circumstances.

For many years, libraries have relied on line-item budgets and simple formulas tied to book stock for budgeting purposes. Both Paul B. Kantor and Jerry D. Campbell have sounded the alarm regarding traditional library budgetary practices and the consequences of these practices as libraries address the demands of new services and activities in the information age. In reporting the results of his major cost study of libraries, Kantor stated:

Overall, academic libraries are quite precariously situated to cope with either a major shift to nonprint media or another fundamental change in the materials to which libraries provide access. The linkage between holdings and budget has provided a comfortable mode of operation for years. Coupled with the general similarity in service mix at various libraries, it has permitted libraries to muddle through. As libraries undertake the provision of other types of information service, they will not find it possible to provide needed services with a formula tied to book stock. The economic viewpoint of libraries must switch from a curatorial, warehousing focus to a focus on the provision of services. The most important tool for understanding of the relations between costs and services is the determination of unit costs.[21]

Campbell also has looked forward to the questions surrounding the costs of new technologies and services. He has stated:

The lesson of the past two decades is clear—nothing will change unless library budgets change. If we have hopes and dreams for vital and dynamic library organizations in the information age and we do not pave the way for them with resources already within our command, they will forever remain in the realm of aspirations. Since we have lost time and a certain advantage, it is also clear that minor adjustments in the nature of the library budgets will not suffice. We require a new vision altogether of the nature of our budgets and the library reality that they will bring into being. In the wake of the revolution in the production of information, our response must be revolutionary . . . . Research libraries require a change of larger magnitude, a change that decreases staff expenditures, that puts greater resources into information and access, that provides better tools.[22]

Budget Process

The budget is actually part of a larger management cycle. This financial management cycle may be conceived of as a wheel that moves from planning and programming to budgeting to operating and measuring to reporting and evaluating which is, in turn, the input for planning and programming.[23] In this cycle, the library is most likely to interact with the parent institution during two phases: the budgeting phase and the reporting phase.

Most institutions require a formal presentation of the budget, certainly in writing, but often in the form of "budget hearings." It is in these circumstances that the library has the opportunity to present its programs and their price tags to the university decision makers. It is also an opportunity to share the vision for the library's future and the steps needed to move toward that future. Budget presentations developed for administrators may also be viewed as a tool for keeping users informed. A summary of the information presented at a budget hearing may be made available to faculty, students, and staff, and discussion on the priorities can be invited. Martin suggests that a budget presentation should answer three questions:

1. What activities are to be carried out?
2. What resources are required to carry out these activities?
3. What will the results be and how will they be measured?[24]

In answering these questions it is important to present the budget very clearly so that it can be easily understood. It is also important to provide sufficient documentation of how the figures were developed so that the effects of proposed reductions to the requested budget can be tracked and demonstrated, if necessary. Sally F. Williams recommends four "Ss" for budget presentations:

keep it Simple
keep it Salient
keep it Scrupulous
pull no Surprises"[25]

In her discussion of these rules, Williams stress the importance of two things: being honest in how the numbers are developed and documented, and keeping good channels of communication with university administrators all during the year, not just at budget time, so that the library's goals and the university's goals are complementary and not contradictory.

The second opportunity that the library has to present its "case" to the university is during the reporting and evaluation phase of the financial management cycle. During this time, the library can show what it achieved during the year and how it used the financial resources to accomplish the priorities established in the budget. At this time, the cost figures developed for each program during the budget preparation and presentation phase will be tested for accuracy and realism. Also at this time the library may see whether it actually followed its stated priorities in expending funds. Ideally, in the reporting and evaluation phase, the library establishes the credibility of its budget process and lays the groundwork for future budget requests.

Evaluation and reporting of the library's financial status should not be a once-a-year thing, even if that is all that is required by the parent institution. Within the library, the monitoring and interpretation of the financial data gathered on a regular (usually monthly) basis should be reported at least quarterly to library senior staff and administration. Popular versions of these reports can be shared with user advisory committees on a formal or informal basis. These reports should include both what has happened financially and what is anticipated to be needed during the rest of the budget year. Duncan McKay described the key features of the financial reports that should be available to the library:

> *timely*: reports are needed shortly after the period to which they refer, not months later when it will be too late to take action to solve any financial problems highlighted;
> *accurate*: all reports should be auditable, e.g. the first level cost center report should be supported by detailed listings of transactions allocated to the cost center concerned;
> *relevant*: reports should only contain information of use to those receiving the report;
> *cost effective*: reports should not be generated where their cost exceeds the financial benefits of having the reported information.[26]

Timely, reliable, relevant, cost-effective management reports enable those charged with accomplishing the libraries' objectives within the resources provided to regularly assess progress toward these goals and make whatever midcourse corrections are necessary to end the year in sound financial shape.

Analysis and reporting of the library's financial status is the basis for evaluation of the library's programs. The management reports may be used to determine if the library is accomplishing its priorities and may indicate the costs of accomplishing those priorities. They can be used to answer questions such as: if library priorities are not being met, is it because adequate resources were not made available, or because estimates of the cost of meeting that priority were poorly identified; or are the finances adequate, but interest in the priority is low or technology needed to support the priority is unavailable? It is only through analysis of the finances and the activity together that effective planning can take place, and funds can be allocated or reallocated to meet goals.

The introduction of document delivery services may illustrate how financial analysis may be used for evaluation of the library's programs. If users complain that a document delivery service is not working effectively, analysis may indicate the cause. Perhaps the library did not allocate adequate funds to cover the fees charged by other libraries for document delivery, thus irritating users who must pay to borrow. Alternatively, the start-up costs for equipment and training of staff may have been underestimated, resulting in inefficient service. Or finally, library staff do not support the document delivery effort so that, in spite of adequate funding, users are not being encouraged to avail themselves of the new service. Financial analysis will help the library and users understand why the service is not operating as planned and what can be done to correct it.

Challenges Facing User-centered Libraries

Up to this point, this chapter has focused on the process skills needed for management of the library's finances: establishing the mission and goals of the library, budget planning, and the budget process. These are universal financial management skills that are applied to the specific problems of libraries. At the present time, there appear to be three ma-

jor challenges for academic libraries to which the financial management tools described previously may be applied. These are: ownership
versus access, funding technology, and fees for services. Each of these
issues is of major interest to users of the library. From the users' perspective, these issues are potentially positive or negative, so it is important to involve users in the decisions and goal-setting around each of
the challenges.

Ownership versus Access

For most of library history, the focus of work has been on the ownership of materials. Much of the literature concerning library funding
revolves around the resources available to buy books and journals. There
are never enough. The cancellation of serial subscriptions is fodder for
research, editorials, and radical proposals. The question, in the long
run, may not be one of ownership, but of access. Barbara Buckner
Higginbotham and Sally Bowdoin have pointed out that "the two events
that have most strongly dictated the shift of emphasis from ownership
to access are the spiraling costs of journal subscriptions and the decline
of the American dollar in the foreign markets where many scholarly
periodicals are published."[27]

Ownership requires: (1) identifying, (2) ordering, (3) receiving,
(4) cataloging, (5) storing, (6) circulating. Each of these steps has
considerable cost.[28] One of the largest is that of storage. Recent studies
suggest that library space currently costs $125 per square foot to
construct.[29] How do these costs compare to the alternatives, such as
resource-sharing or electronic access?

Resource-sharing, in the form of cooperative collection
development or consortium membership, involves all of the preceding
steps, plus the costs of either copying or transporting. Although there
are not many existing reports of cost-benefit analysis for access versus
ownership, the data from a few are both suggestive and demonstrate
models that any library may use to conduct its own analysis. In 1989, the
Virginia Tech Library reported the total cost of purchasing and
shelving a monograph to be $106 each, and for serial volumes $181
each.[30] In 1993, Anthony W. Ferguson and Kathleen Kehoe reported
on the costs of ownership versus access (borrowing) for monographs
and journals in the biology, physics, and electrical engineering libraries

at Columbia University. Using the ARL/RLG methodology,[31] they found that the fully loaded (unsubsidized) borrowing costs per document averaged $25.90.[32]

> The costs for owning a monograph for its first use were clearly higher than for accessing it when needed. The purchase price, and the acquisitions processing and cataloging costs associated with the purchase of the 235 monographs borrowed without regard to long term storage and preservation costs would have cost the library $33,370 in 1991 dollars instead of the $6,086 the libraries spent borrowing them. Adding the storage and preservation costs would only add to the cost of ownership.[33]

Their analysis of periodical borrowing indicated that even for journals requested up to ten times, it was 21 to 31 times more expensive to own than to borrow.[34] Finally, A. Craig Hawbaker and Cynthia K. Wagner reported on a comparison for the cost of ownership versus online access for business periodicals. They found that although the cost of the full-text database was higher ($35,374 for the database versus $30,660 for the subscriptions), the number of titles available increased from 242 to 513, resulting in a cost of $127 per title for the printed subscriptions versus $69 per title for the online full-text subscriptions.[35] Although these cost-benefit analyses are not conclusive, they are suggestive. Each library should look at the ownership versus access question in light of its own costs. Using the ARL/RLG interlibrary loan cost methodology would provide consistent data for the library, which could then also be compared to other libraries.

The costs of owning materials have not been known to library users, who, if they think about them at all, tie only the purchase price to the item. Even then, faculty tend to underestimate these costs: for serials, the institutional purchase price may be many times the cost of an individual subscription. As the ownership versus access debate has grown, libraries have begun to study the real costs of ownership. Charles A. Schwartz has suggested a serial cancellation model that uses a cost-per-use analysis process to evaluate high-cost/low-use periodicals coupled with a "top-down deliberation and bottom-up review" that includes all stakeholders.[36] Library users (as well as librarians themselves) should be informed of the full costs of ownership of materials and the full costs of borrowing. It is only with this information at hand that librarians and library users can make the difficult decisions about the trade-offs between access and ownership. Library users, in the consultative processes described earlier, can help the library make the decisions and can share responsibility for the decisions by communicating with their peer groups on the campus.

Funding Technology

The questions surrounding the funding of technology relate to many parts of the library's traditional budget structure. Is technology "instead of" or "in addition to"? If instead of, instead of what? Instead of books and journals? Instead of staff? Instead of a new addition to the building? Maurice Glicksman describes the challenges of establishing budget priorities for technology as follows:

> A major problem in the introduction of new technology is the difficulty of assigning priority in the library budget for the costs. . . . In a certain sense, these costs are opportunity costs which provide for significant improvements in operation, including service to the scholarly community. If it is clear that the new technology leads to the ultimate planned linkage, there is little doubt that the scholarly community can be more supportive of the sacrifice needed to achieve this.[37]

Electronic access has many forms, each with its associated costs. CD ROMs, which most commonly replace paper access tools, increasingly contain the actual content. Should libraries continue to purchase paper copies or rely on the electronic versions? Using CD-ROMs in networks allows multiuser access at the same time. Will simultaneous multiuser access allow for the purchase of just one copy of the material?

Materials available on the World Wide Web give the illusion of being free. The substantial costs of the information superhighway appear to be invisible to most college and university users. In addition, what was originally the preserve of the Defense Department and major universities is now public property available to all. Fee-based information services already exist on the Web, and their use rates are growing. Arnold Hirshorn describes the commercialization of the Internet and its impact on libraries. He concludes that:

> Internet commercialization will change the strategic directions for library customer services. Librarians typically have given away expertise for free. The Internet is creating a new venue for fee-based access and retrieval information services that could provide the necessary capital to continue funding high-cost technology. Ultimately, commercialization of the Internet may be what makes libraries more expensive, more lucrative, and, ironically, more customer-service oriented because it will be the marketplace that will determine which services are essential."[38]

Staff now spend time organizing the physical collection: cataloging, shelving, shelf-reading, binding, repair. How do these costs compare to the costs of maintaining the computer equipment, networks, CD ROMs? How do they compare to the costs of organizing and creating finding tools on the Web? Libraries are only beginning to do the cost-benefit analysis of ownership versus access, but these studies need to be expanded to include cost/benefit analysis of doing library business on the Web and other Internet resources. Users will need to be consulted to determine what Web-based services they want and need, what they are currently paying or are willing to pay to get these services, and the trade-offs they are willing to have the library make to support the services.

Fees for Services

Closely tied to the discussions of ownership versus access and funding technology are the discussions of fees for services. The library world has long viewed information as an entitlement and considered access to information to be governed by laws of equity.[39] However, library funding has not been able to keep up with the growing demands for new and technologically advanced services, nor even to maintain the status quo in terms of the library materials budget. As was discussed earlier, without careful analysis of the library's funding in relation to its priorities, "library administrators are faced with a dilemma: maintain no fee policies and deny users access to useful services, or charge fees and disenfranchise those who can not pay."[40] Despite this dilemma, libraries have continued to push costs directly to patrons where it appears that the market will bear such costs. Libraries have long charged for photocopying (or, more recently, printing from a library computer station), practices that are acceptable because no one is directly denied information, just the opportunity to absorb it in a time and place of one's choosing. More recently, libraries mediate charges for a database provided by an external vendor, but accessible from library workstations. The costs of interlibrary loan are either charged to the patron or absorbed, depending on the cooperative arrangements in which a library participates. In these instances and others, what is lacking is a careful and complete analysis of the costs and the benefits of the charging schemes. Often overlooked are the actual costs of billing, collecting the money, and reporting to the parent institution. Equally ignored are the salaries of the staff who mediate the activities and the overhead costs within the library that allow the "for-fee" service to operate. The debate on fee versus free is far from over, but it could do with a breath of fresh air in the form of well-constructed financial studies and a review of the priorities of the library.

Conclusion

Money is a tool for helping a library accomplish its goals and objectives. The process of applying financial resources to the priorities of the library is the budget process. The budget is simply a plan for how to best use the dollars available to meet program needs. There are no simple solutions to library budgeting, one approach does not fit all libraries, let alone all academic libraries. Each library must establish its priorities within the context of the institution it serves and the users who rely on it.

The budget process is one that has to be undertaken at least annually, but budget reviews should be ongoing to adapt to changing financial circumstances and to take advantage of unexpected opportunity.

Budgetary decisions, once made, may need to be revisited. All budgeting involves trade offs, and budgetary decisions in higher education are always made with incomplete data. Flexibility in budgetary thinking is a must.

Glicksman has suggested that there are three areas in which the library must establish priorities in the coming decades:

- how to deal efficiently with the growing quantity of scholarly material;
- how to respond to the deteriorating quality of the form of materials held;
- how to guide the introduction of new technology to maximize utility and minimize cost[41]

Each of these areas represents a major current or future cost for libraries. These are not separate problems but, instead, must be addressed together within the context of library financial planning. To move forward on any of these issues requires that each library establish priorities for its human and financial resources. In one form or another, all of these areas will directly impact users' satisfaction with the library. Users of the library are important sources of information for priority-setting and budget planning. Consultation within the library, within the college or university, and within the national library community will be necessary. However, until libraries are able to carefully analyze the real costs of doing business, tie them to the priority services provided, and act on that information, they will not be putting people first.

Notes

1. Hugh C. Atkinson, "Response to 'Creating the Conditions for Change' by Donald P. Ely," in *Changing Times Changing Libraries: 22nd Allerton Park Institute* (Urbana-Champaign: Univ. of Illinois Graduate School of Library Science, 1978), 148–49.

2. Stephen E. Atkins, *The Academic Library in the American University* (Chicago: ALA, 1991), 80.

3. Michael D. Cooper, "Economic Trends in Academic Libraries," in Martin M. Cummings, *The Economics of Research Libraries* (Washington, D.C.: Council on Library Resources, 1986), 146.

4. Frank W. Goudy, "Academic Libraries and the Six Percent Solution: A Twenty Year Financial Overview," *Journal of Academic Librarianship* 19 (Sept. 1993): 212–15.

5. John M. Budd, "A Critique of Customer and Commodity," *College & Research Libraries* 58 (July 1997): 312.

6. Marvin R. Weisbord and Sandra Janoff, *Future Search: An Action Guide to Finding Common Ground in Organizations and Communities* (San Francisco: Berrett-Koehler, 1995).

7. Stephen Covey, *The Seven Habits of Highly Effective People: Restoring the Character Ethic* (New York: Simon & Schuster, 1989).

8. Ann E. Prentice, *Financial Planning for Libraries* 2nd ed. (Metuchen, N.J.: Scarecrow Pr., 1996).

9. Madeline J. Daubert, *Financial Management for Small and Medium-Sized Libraries* (Chicago: ALA, 1993).

10. Richard J. Talbot, "Financing the Academic Library" in *Priorities for Academic Libraries*, ed. Thomas J. Galvin and Beverly P. Lynch, New Directions in Higher Education, no. 39 (San Francisco: Josey-Bass, 1992), 35–44.

11. Murray S. Martin, *Academic Library Budgets* (Greenwich, Conn.: JAI Pr., 1993), 30.

12. Sherman Hayes and Don Brown, "The Library as a Business: Mapping the Pervasiveness of Financial Relationships in Today's Library," *Library Trends* 42, no. 3, (winter 1994): 416.

13. Duncan McKay, *Effective Financial Planning for Library and Information Services* (London: ASLIB, The Association for Information Management, 1995), 21.

14. Prentice, *Financial Planning for Libraries*, 60–65.

15. Ibid., 67.

16. Martin, *Academic Library Budgets*, 23.

17. Betty J. Turok, "Taking the Library Budget out of the 'Twilight Zone'" *Library Administration & Management* 3 (spring 1989): 65.

18. William K. Black, "The Budget as a Planning Tool," *Journal of Library Administration* 18, no. 3/4, (1993): 175.

19. Daubert, *Financial Management for Small and Medium-Sized Libraries*.

20. Martin, *Academic Library Budgets*.

21. Paul B. Kantor, "The Relation between Costs and Services at Academic Libraries," in *Financing Information Services: Problems, Changing Approaches, and New Opportunities for Academic and Research Libraries*, eds.

Peter Spyers-Duran and Thomas W. Mann (Westport, Conn.: Green-wood Pr., 1985), 73.

22. Jerry D. Campbell, "Academic Library Budgets: Changing 'the Sixty-Forty Split,'" *Library Administration & Management*, 3, (spring 1989): 78.

23. Daubert, *Financial Management for Small and Medium-Sized Libraries*, 6.

24. Martin, *Academic Library Budgets*, 112.

25. Sally F. Williams, "Budget Justification: Closing the Gap between Request and Result," *Library Resources & Technical Services*, 28, (Apr./June 1984): 131.

26. McKay, *Effective Financial Planning for Library and Information Services*, 30.

27. Barbra Buckner Higginbotham and Sally Bowdoin, *Access versus Assets: A Comprehensive Guide to Resource Sharing for Academic Libraries* (Chicago: ALA, 1993), 9.

28. Charles B. Lowry, "Resource Sharing or Cost Shifting?: The Unequal Burden of Cooperative Cataloging and ILL in Networks," *College & Research Libraries* 51 (Jan. 1990): 11–19.

29. Higginbotham and Bowdoin, *Access versus Assets*, 15.

30. Paul M. Gherman and Lynn Scott Cochrane, "Developing and Using Unit Costs: The Virginia Tech Experience," *Library Administration & Management* 3 (spring 1989): 93–96.

31. Marilyn M. Roche, *ARL/RLG Interlibrary Loan Cost Study: A Joint Effort by the Association of Research Libraries and the Research Libraries Group* (Washington, D.C.: Association of Research Libraries, 1993).

32. Anthony W. Ferguson and Kathleen Kehoe, "Access vs Ownership: What Is Most Cost Effective in the Sciences," *Journal of Library Administration* 19 (1993): 98.

33. Ibid., 91.

34. Ibid., 95.

35. A. Craig Hawbaker and Cynthia K. Wagner, "Periodical Ownership versus Fulltext Online Access: A Cost-Benefit Analysis," *Journal of Academic Librarianship* 22 (Mar. 1996): 105–9.

36. Charles A. Schwartz, "Restructuring Serials Management to Generate New Resources and Service—With Commentaries on Restructurings at Three Institutions," *College & Research Libraries* 59 (Mar. 1998): 115–24.

37. Maurice Glicksman, "Supporting Scholarship in Universities: A Response to the Growing Costs of Information Services," in *Financing Information Ser-*

vices: Problems, Changing Approaches, and New Opportunities for Academic and Research Libraries, ed. Peter Spyers-Duran and Thomas W. Mann (Westport, Conn.: Greenwood Pr., 1985), 67.

38. Arnold Hirshon, "Running with the Red Queen: Breaking New Habits to Survive in the Virtual World," *Advances in Librarianship* 20 (1996): 19–20.

39. Carlton C. Rochell, "The Knowledge Business: Economic Issues of Access to Bibliographic Information," *College & Research Libraries* 46 (Jan. 1985): 6.

40. S. Michael Malinconico, "Technology and the Academic Workplace," *Library Administration & Management* 5 (winter 1991): 27.

41. Glicksman, "Supporting Scholarship in Universities, 60.

Conclusion

Although technology is a powerful tool, it is people—librarians and staff—who build user-centered libraries. Technology has enabled us to give better service than ever before, but we have not used technology to redefine services in the systemwide manner that is needed if users are to be fully served. Instead, we continue to organize our libraries around traditional functions. In analyzing the contributions of the chapter authors, the editors came to believe that the time has come to reevaluate the functional approach to library organization. Specialization by function is an artifact of the past when libraries were constrained by the physical limitations of the tools of the trade (centralized acquisitions and serial files, the card catalog and authority files, circulation records, etc.). Technology has eliminated the restrictions imposed by a requirement for on-site tools. The close and interdependent relationship among reference, instruction and training, cataloging, circulation, collection development, and interlibrary loan makes the separation of these activities arbitrary.[1] Users have never been interested in the functional distinctions made by librarians. From their perspective, the issue was one of access to information, independent of its physical form, its location, or how libraries gather and store it.

In writing this concluding commentary, the editors sought the advice of Kathleen Kluegel, past president of Reference and User Services Association of ALA. Kluegel commented that "in thinking about the topic 'patrons come first,' I created a mental model of the library as overlapping circles of service, with the patron standing at the epicenter of each circle. Some service circles overlapped with one another just a little bit, while others shared a lot of space, rather like a Venn diagram."

Functional organizations tend to obscure the overlap across circles; they stifle collaboration and thwart communication. The chapters on reference service and circulation provide examples of the interrelatedness of traditional functions. In the chapter on reference service, John C. Stalker describes the informal triage system that exists in every library and Lynn Wiley and John Harer depict the important role circulation staff plays in this system. However, despite this informal system, our functional organizations block real collaboration between circulation and reference, even though, as Kathleen Kluegel says, "a well designed triage system, combined with well-trained staff members, can result in an effective reference service model." We cannot begin to design user-friendly systems until we stop compartmentalizing activities.

We can contrast functional organizations with the user-centered organization that Lizabeth A. Wilson defines in her "gateway library." She describes a structure that allows for project development, fosters collaboration, creates a safe haven for ideas, and relies on expertise from within and outside the library. In this organization, services to undergraduates are the goal and technology the tool. This is a model that academic libraries could apply to the library as a whole.

Michael Gorman identifies three keys to quality service: vision, attitudinal change, and user-friendly systems. The authors have discussed a way to develop user-friendly systems. Improved communications (both internal and external), education and training, and institution-wide user-centered goals nurture vision and attitudinal changes. Communicating is not just a matter of telling; it is also a matter of listening with an open mind. Education and training are significant for librarians, staff, and users. Librarians and staff must continually learn new technology and make training for users accessible from remote locations because users increasingly access our services in their dorm rooms, offices, and from other remote sites. User-centered goals result from leadership, teamwork, and an understanding of user needs.

Ignorance of user needs creates barriers to service. User needs assessment is a basic tool for any library with the goal of putting users first.[2] We can all benefit from a knowledge of research methods, moving beyond a sole reliance on questionnaires and transaction logs to greater use of observation and interview. Learning about our users' needs is the first step, but meeting them is a bit more complicated. As Wilson and Stephen E. Atkins and Patricia F. Stenstrom illustrate, not all users want the same service, and as Dale S. Montanelli points out, we must balance conflicting needs with available resources. However, we can not and should not pit one user group against another.

As a profession, we librarians have simultaneously adapted to change but have clung to structures and practices that are no longer meaningful. We worry about the future of libraries because we do not appreciate the value of the services we offer. We need to stop looking inward and look outward to our users so that we help them locate, evaluate, and interpret the vast information resources now available.

Notes

1. For another discussion of the same theme, see Ross Atkinson, "Access, Ownership, and the Future of Collection Development" in *Collection Manage ment and Development Issues in an Electronic Era*, ed. Peggy Johnson and Bonnie MacEwan (Chicago: ALA, 1994), 92–109.

2. David Nicholas, *Assessing Information Needs: Tools and Te chniques.* (London: Aslib, 1996).

Biographies

Stephen E. Atkins is associate university librarian for collection management at the Evans General Libraries at Texas A&M University. He was previously head of collection development at the Evans General Libraries and a political science subject specialist at the University of Illinois Library at Urbana-Champaign. Dr. Atkins is an eclectic author writing on arms control and disarmament, library science, terrorism, and atomic energy. His book, *The Academic Library in the American University*, was published in 1991. His doctorate in French history and library science degree are from the University of Iowa. E-mail: s-atkins@tamu.edu.

Richard M. Dougherty is professor emeritus in the School of Information at the University of Michigan. He formerly served as director of libraries at Michigan from 1978-1988, and at the University of California, Berkeley, from 1972-1978. He earned his advanced degrees in librarianship from Rutgers University. Professor Dougherty is a former editor of both *College and Research Libraries* and the *Journal of Academic Librarianship*. He is currently editor of *Library Issues* and has published numerous articles, editorials, and monographs. He is also president of Dougherty and Associates, a consulting firm that specializes in helping organizations develop and implement change management strategies. E-mail: rmdoughe@umich.edu.

Michael Gorman is dean of library services at the Henry Madden Library, California State University, Fresno. From 1977 to 1988, he worked at the University of Illinois at Urbana-Champaign as, successively, director of technical services, director of general services, and acting university librarian. He has taught in library schools in his native Britain and in the United States, most recently at the University of California, Berkeley. Mr. Gorman is the first editor of the *Anglo American Cataloging Rules,* second edition (1978), and of the revision of that work (1988). His most recent book, published by ALA in 1997, is titled *Our Singular Strengths: Meditations for Librarians.* Mr. Gorman is author of more than 100 articles in professional and scholarly journals. He is a fellow of the [British] Library Association, the 1979 recipient of the Margaret Mann Citation, and the 1992 recipient of the Melvil Dewey Medal. E-mail: michael_gorman@csufresno.edu.

John B. Harer is currently the head of education reference for the Sterling C. Evans Library at Texas A&M University, and formerly head of access services for Texas A&M University libraries. He holds an MSLS in library science from the Graduate School of Library Science at Clarion University of PA and an MPA in public administration from the University of Baltimore. Mr. Harer has served on the Library Management and Administration section's Circulation Services Committee for many years and has authored several articles on circulation aspects and interlibrary loan. He was also a member of the ALA Intellectual Freedom Committee and has written two monographs on censorship and intellectual freedom. E-mail: jbharer@tamu.edu.

Patricia McCandless is assistant director for public services at The Ohio State University Libraries. Prior to joining the faculty at Ohio State, she worked at the University of Illinois at Urbana-Champaign Library for twenty years in a variety of positions, the last as head of a department library and assistant director for the Life Science Libraries. Her research interests include evaluation of service and assessment of user needs. E-mail: mccandless.1@osu.edu.

Dale S. Montanelli is an associate professor of human and community development in the College of Agricultural, Consumer, and Environmental Sciences at the University of Illinois at Urbana-Champaign. She received a bachelor's degree from Michigan State University, a master's in library science and a master's and a doctorate in psychology from the University of Illinois at Urbana-Champaign. Dr. Montanelli has served as associate director of the Illinois Cooperative Extension Service and director of administrative services in the University Library. She has been active in both extension and library professional organizations, including the Association of Leadership Educators and the Library Administration and Management division of ALA. Dr. Montanelli's research interests include the interaction of humans with their environments, both physical and social. She has published and presented papers in the areas of financial, facilities, and human resources management. E-mail: montanel@uiuc.edu.

Stephen J. Smith is the acting OCLC cataloging librarian and assistant professor of library administration, University of Illinois at Urbana-Champaign. He earned his BS from the University of Wisconsin and MS in library and information science from the University of Illinois. Mr. Smith has been a member of the Forum on Natural History Cataloging Issues of the Association for Library Collections and Technical Services of the ALA. He has written on the topic of training in *Technical Services Quarterly* and has led training for the Illinois OCLC User's Group. E-mail: stephenj@ux1.cso.uiuc.edu.

John C. Stalker received his MA and PhD in English from the University of North Carolina at Chapel Hill, and between the two earned his MLS from the same institution. He has been head of reference at The Ohio State University and Boston College, in addition to serving as head of public services at Atlanta University and director at the University of Scranton. His publications include articles on measuring and analyzing quality reference service. Other research interests lie in readability studies, especially as they relate to textbooks and children's literature. E-mail: jcs@niagra.edu.

Patricia F. Stenstrom is associate professor emerita at the University of Illinois at Urbana-Champaign where she also received her MS in library science and spent most of her long professional career. She is the former library and information science librarian and also taught in the Graduate School of Library and Information Science. Professor Stenstrom is author of a number of articles relating to "library literature" and complied the "library and information" section of the *Guide to Reference Books*, 11th edition, edited by Robert Baley, 1995. She has been chair of both the ACRL Discussion Group Librarians of Library Science Collections and the Library Research Round Table's Library and Information Task Force. E-mail: stenstrom@dbstech.com.

Lynn Wiley has been active in access services for most of her library career. Her previous positions include head of access at Tufts University, Wessell Library; access services librarian at the University of Massachusetts, Boston; and head of circulation, Boston College O'Neill Library. Currently, she heads up the Illinois Research and Reference Center of the University of Illinois at Urbana Champaign. She received her MSLS from the University of North Carolina, Chapel Hill. She is active in several ALA committees including the RUSA MOUSS ILL Committee. E-mail: l-wiley@uiuc.edu.

Juliet Williams received her MS from School of Information at the University of Michigan.

Lizabeth A. (Betsy) Wilson is associate director of libraries for public services at the University of Washington. She has been coadministrator of the award-winning UWired program at the University of Washington since its inception in 1994. Prior to joining the University of Washington in 1992, Ms. Wilson was the assistant director of libraries for Undergraduate and Instructional Services at the University of Illinois at Urbana-Champaign. She has held numerous leadership roles in ALA and ACRL, including chair of the Instruction Section, member of ALA Council, and candidate for ACRL vice-president/president-elect (1999). She is the recipient of the 1995 Miriam Dudley Instruction Librarian Award and a prolific author and speaker on teaching and learning in libraries, collaboration, information technology, and assessment and evaluation. Ms. Wilson holds a B.A. in Art History and German from Northwestern University (1977) and an MS in library and information science from the University of Illinois at Urbana-Champaign (1978). E-mail: betsyw@u.washington.edu.

Index